The
Walker
Art
Gallery

The
Walker
Art
Gallery

Produced by Liverpool University Press
for
National Museums Liverpool
127 Dale Street
Liverpool
L2 2JH

ISBN 978-1-902700-47-2

Printed and bound in Poland by Opolgraf

Walker
Art Gallery

Contents

Foreword

The Walker Art Gallery is famous for the world-class quality and variety of its collections. One day's visit is barely long enough to enjoy all the riches on offer, but we hope that this guide will provide a memorable souvenir of the artistic treasures on view. The guide acts as an introduction to the collections, with around 150 pictures of artworks covering all the periods of art on display, from the medieval to the present day.

The earliest collections begin with European fine and decorative art from 1200, encompassing the Renaissance and Baroque periods, and include masterpieces by Simone Martini, Rembrandt and Poussin, with a notable and controversial addition by subversive contemporary artist Banksy. Extensive collections of 18th- and 19th-century British painting and sculpture include paintings by Hogarth and Stubbs, and famous Pre-Raphaelite works by Rossetti and Millais. Yeames' *And When Did You Last See Your Father?* retains its longstanding popularity, and is one of the world's most frequently reproduced Victorian paintings. Later 19th-century art movements, including European Impressionism, are also represented. Galleries of British modern and contemporary art include works by winners of the John Moores Painting Prize such as David Hockney and Peter Doig.

Called 'Walky Through Gallery' by John Lennon, the Walker Art Gallery holds a special place in the heart of Liverpudlians, and is the result of private generosity and public idealism. A founding gift from Sir Andrew Barclay Walker enabled the building of the Gallery, which opened in 1877. Many of the great families and individuals of Liverpool have made, and continue to make, important gifts and donations. Molly Tomlinson's bequest enabled us in 2011 to redisplay British art from 1880 to 1950.

This redesigned guide builds on an existing guidebook developed by a team that included Edward Morris, Alex Kidson, Xanthe Brooke, Joseph Sharples, Robin Emmerson, Frank Milner, Pete Betts and Sharon Trotter. This new book adapts that earlier publication to take into account changes in the Walker Art Gallery's collections and displays. It includes new highlights and updated information. We are indebted to Xanthe Brooke, Laura MacCulloch, Lucy Gardner, Sandra Penketh, Ann Bukantas, Karen Miller and Angela Barlow for their hard work to produce a modern and accessible guide to the collections and the Gallery.

Many of the works of art featured here were purchases made with the assistance of donations from individuals, companies or funding bodies. We acknowledge the consistent support of the Art Fund, in particular. We would like to dedicate this book to all our donors past and present, in gratitude for their generosity, and for the pleasure and inspiration given to all our visitors.

Dr David Fleming OBE, Director
National Museums Liverpool

Introduction:
The History of the Gallery and its Collections

The construction of the Walker Art Gallery was not begun until 1874, but some of its most important paintings had been on public display in Liverpool since 1819. In that year 37 small paintings were hung in the Liverpool Royal Institution. They had been bought in 1816 from the bankruptcy auction of Liverpool's most eminent citizen, William Roscoe, notable as a historian, collector, botanist, poet, philanthropist, Radical politician, banker and lawyer. Roscoe had always wanted his large collection of paintings, drawings and prints to be of public benefit. His friends and associates among the Nonconformist Radical merchants of Liverpool managed to save this small part of his collection of paintings from dispersal. The belief among collectors, manufacturers and artists that public collections would improve and refine taste and quality lay behind the creation of most museums and art galleries in 19th-century Britain and this is probably the first practical, public and explicit expression of the idea.

The display of Roscoe's paintings was improved by the construction in 1840-43 of a new purpose-built art gallery next to the Royal Institution's premises in Colquitt Street. It had an upper floor with sophisticated lighting for pictures and a lower floor for casts and sculpture. Soon more works of art were acquired – mainly Old Master paintings – by purchase and gift on a modest scale. The Royal Institution was run by and for its proprietors, but the general public were admitted in return for a fee or, occasionally, as at the art gallery on some Mondays, free of charge. Despite its events programme and publications the new art gallery did not prove very popular and generated only a modest regular income. In 1850-51 negotiations began between the Royal Institution and the Liverpool Town Council about the transfer of the Institution and its art collections to the Town Council, which had by then been authorised by Parliament to provide museums and art galleries at the expense of its ratepayers. The Institution's proprietors, however, wanted to retain some control over its collections and educational programme, even after the takeover by the Council, and to this the Council would not agree.

After the failure of these negotiations the Council built the William Brown Library and Museum (now World Museum) between 1857 and 1860 but took little more direct interest in providing an art gallery, although it slowly continued to acquire paintings and sculptures for its own collections. They were to be the nucleus of the future 'Gallery of Arts' and were mostly placed temporarily in its new Museum and Library buildings. In 1871 the first Liverpool Autumn Exhibition was arranged by the Council in the Museum. This was an exhibition of paintings by living artists for sale – a Liverpool

opposite: The Liverpool Autumn Exhibition of 1882 held in the Gallery

version of the London-based Royal Academy Summer Exhibitions. The Autumn Exhibitions were very successful, yielding a substantial profit. This encouraged the Council to spend £500 on buying pictures mainly from the exhibition for the still unbuilt art gallery. Similar exhibitions were held in the following years and more paintings purchased until in 1873 Andrew Barclay Walker, having been elected Mayor of Liverpool, gave £20,000 towards the building of a public art gallery which was to bear his name. The architects were local men, Henry H Vale and Cornelius Sherlock.

Walker was a Conservative brewer and, although not notable as a collector or patron of art, he built public houses in Liverpool of considerable architectural quality and gave generously to many local good causes. No doubt this was partly to improve the public image of brewing and of alcohol in general at a time when the teetotal temperance movement, largely sponsored by his political adversaries, the Liberals, was growing in strength. The Walker Art Gallery opened to the public in 1877, primarily to house the annual temporary Liverpool Autumn Exhibitions which had been dislocating the Museum's displays since 1871. The profits from these exhibitions continued to be spent on increasing the size of the permanent collection, which by 1885 included some 360 works of art. The source of this funding encouraged the Council to buy almost exclusively contemporary British paintings and sculpture, mostly from the Autumn Exhibitions, but they also bought often adventurous paintings by Continental European artists, such as the Symbolist Swiss painter, Segantini.

The Hanging Committee at the 1891 Liverpool Autumn Exhibition, including the artist Whistler, seated left.

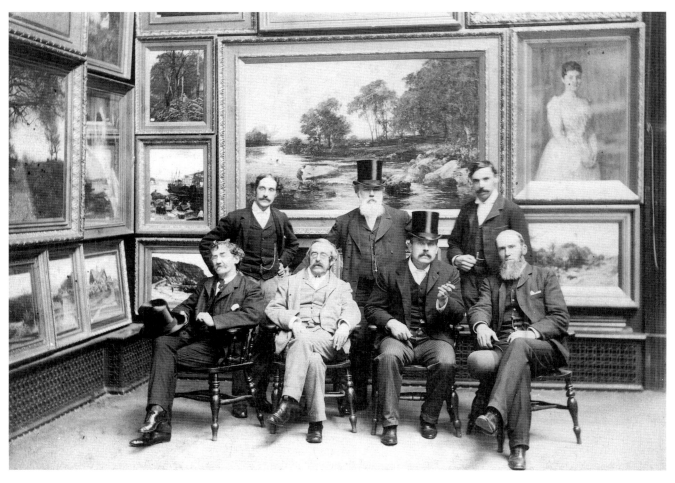

During World War II the Ministry of Food used the Walker for the issuing of food ration books.

It was the growth of the permanent collection which encouraged the Council to enlarge the Gallery in 1882, and again Walker paid the entire cost (£11,500). Liverpool could now claim to have the finest art gallery outside London and attendance figures peaked at 610,779 in 1880 (2,349 each day). In 1893 most of the paintings owned by the Liverpool Royal Institution were placed on long-term loan for display at the Walker Art Gallery. With the decline in vitality of the Autumn Exhibitions partly due to the death of their main organiser, Philip Rathbone, in 1895 the permanent collection rather than loan exhibitions became the principal feature of the Gallery.

A number of important gifts, mainly of 19th-century art by British and Continental artists such as Watts and Rodin, were received from James Smith and George Audley in the 1920s and 1930s, and in 1929 for the first time a contribution from the rates (£750) was made to the picture purchase fund, which before then had been dependent on gifts and on the declining profits from the Autumn Exhibitions. Purchasing became less restrained in scope and in the 1930s and 1940s, with Vere Cotton as Chairman of the Libraries, Museums and Arts Committee of Liverpool City Council, and with Frank Lambert as Director of the Gallery, notable 18th-century British works and important Camden Town paintings from the 20th century were acquired. This bolder policy was also assisted by a bequest in 1933 of £20,000 from Lord Wavertree, son of Andrew Barclay Walker.

Sir John Moores and David Hockney at the 1967–68 John Moores Liverpool Exhibition with Hockney's winning painting *Peter Getting Out of Nick's Pool.*

Meanwhile the Gallery was again extended towards the rear and the entrance hall remodelled in 1931–33. The architect was Andrew Thorneley of Briggs and Thorneley, who had designed the Mersey Docks and Harbour Board Offices in 1907. It is noteworthy that the Walker Art Gallery has depended on private generosity both for its buildings and for its collections to a much larger extent than most other British art galleries.

The Gallery closed during the Second World War. It was taken over by the Ministry of Food for the issuing of food ration books and its collections removed to country houses and schools in nearby counties (so unlike the city's museum it did not lose works due to bomb damage). It only reopened in 1951, but in 1948 the Liverpool Royal Institution paintings, already on loan, were formally presented to the Walker. Under Hugh Scrutton as Director, purchasing policy again widened to include Old Master paintings and, from 1961 onwards, French Impressionist and Post-Impressionist paintings, many of which were bought through a special appeal for funds directed to Merseyside industry and commerce. After the War there was a new emphasis on conservation. J Coburn Witherop set up a studio for the conservation of paintings in the Gallery and in 1955 presented the pioneering exhibition of *Cleaned Pictures* from the Walker's collections. In 1957 the biennial John Moores Liverpool Exhibition began under the joint sponsorship of Sir John Moores. Thanks to the John Moores Painting Prize exhibitions the Gallery was able to re-establish its original role of acquiring on a regular basis major examples of British contemporary art. Education was not neglected in the appointment of the Gallery's first full-time Schools Officer in 1957 and, following in the tradition of the Liverpool Royal Institution, detailed scholarly catalogues of the collections began to be written and published.

With the reform of local government in 1973 the Merseyside County Council assumed financial responsibility for the Gallery. Following the abolition of the Council in 1986 the Gallery received national status and central government funding as part of the newly formed National Museums and Galleries on Merseyside (now National Museums Liverpool) along with Sudley House and the Lady Lever Art Gallery, over which the Walker had assumed responsibility in 1945 and 1978 respectively. Cumulatively these three expressions of confidence in the Walker Art Gallery confirmed its role as the leading English art gallery outside London, whose collections range across 800 years from the 12th to the 21st century.

The closure and refurbishment of the Walker Art Gallery began in 1999, as part of National Museums Liverpool's *Into the Future* project. The Gallery reopened in 2002 and now features new temporary exhibition galleries and the Craft and Design gallery, the Walker Art Gallery's first dedicated space for the decorative arts which opened in 2004. The gallery highlights the Walker's extensive decorative arts collection including jewellery, tableware, fashion and furniture. In 2011 the Walker opened its newest gallery, British Art 1880–1950, which explores the transition from Victorian to modern British art by displaying ceramics, drawings, furniture, paintings and sculpture in historical context. A new gallery for younger visitors was launched in 2006. *Big Art for Little Artists* is a space to discover art through looking, touching, listening and doing, and provides a launch pad for discovering the rest of the Gallery's world-famous collections.

Plaque from a Book Cover, 1200–25

French (*Limoges*)

Enamel on copper,
11.3 x 20.5 cm

Presented by Joseph Mayer in 1867; inv. no. M9

Limoges was the principal centre for the production of enamelled metalwork in Europe in the 13th century. The figure of St John the Evangelist suggests that this was intended as the cover for a gospel book.

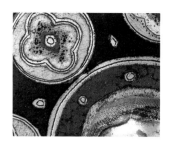

The Walker Art Gallery was not founded with a conscious policy of collecting either medieval or early Renaissance art, and therefore the outstanding quality of this part of the collection is surprising. Most of the works come from two private collections amassed by the 19th-century Liverpool collectors William Roscoe and Joseph Mayer. The two men were keen antiquarians: Mayer collected and studied examples of Roman, Egyptian and medieval artefacts; Roscoe was interested in the history and development of Renaissance art. Both men saw their collections as having an educational role and hoped that the city would benefit from them.

William Roscoe (1753-1831) acquired a large number of the paintings in this part of the collection between 1804 and 1816. He was a successful Liverpool lawyer and Radical politician, who campaigned against the slave trade, and whose interests included history, pottery, botany, poetry and art. Remarkably, he was a self-educated man much influenced by the example of the Renaissance patrons – he wrote a notable history of Lorenzo de' Medici in 1796. Roscoe was eager to promote cultural development in the expanding commercial centre of Liverpool. He was active in the formation of both the Liverpool Royal Institution and the Athenaeum Library, and became a significant collector, starting first with books and then extending his interest to prints and finally 'primitive' – that is 14th- and 15th-century – paintings and drawings.

Unfortunately, his bankruptcy in 1816 forced Roscoe to sell off his collection. After the sale a small group of Roscoe's paintings found their way into the collection of the Liverpool Royal Institution, mainly due to the determined spirit of William Rathbone, radical merchant and close friend of Roscoe. Here the collection was extended and finally given to the Walker Art Gallery by the Institution in 1948. A large part of Roscoe's Renaissance and Baroque drawings collection was bought at the 1816 sale by Charles Blundell (1761-1837), who added it to the large collection of paintings, drawings and sculpture he and his father, Henry (1724-1810), had amassed at Ince Blundell Hall, north of Liverpool. Between 1995 and 1998 several hundred Old Master drawings from this Weld-Blundell collection were bought for the Walker.

Joseph Mayer (1803-86) was born in Newcastle-under-Lyme, Staffordshire. He moved to Liverpool when he was 20 years old. At first he was apprenticed to his brother-in-law Joseph Wordley, a jeweller, but in 1844-45 Mayer set up his own jewellery and silversmith business. It was probably this enterprise which provided him with sufficient funds to finance his passion for collecting. Mayer's interest in antiquities began at an early age and his collection covered a wide range of subjects including Wedgwood pottery, Egyptian and Roman artefacts, English paintings and medieval art. In 1852 Mayer opened a museum in Liverpool's Colquitt Street, using works he had collected as the exhibits. He had become captivated by the displays at the British Museum and wished his fellow citizens of Liverpool to have the same opportunity to view the wonders of the past. As well as setting up the Museum, Mayer was a founder member of the Historic Society of Lancashire and Cheshire, established in 1848, and a Fellow of the Society of Antiquaries. In 1867 Mayer gave his collection to Liverpool Museum. The medieval illuminated manuscripts, ivories and enamels which made up part of this gift are now in the care of the Walker Art Gallery.

Psalter, 1225–50

South German

Vellum, 25.7 x 18.5 cm

Presented by Joseph Mayer in 1867; inv. no. M12004

Psalters are service books containing all the Psalms and prayers. They were used by the clergy from the 9th century but became increasingly popular with lay readers from the 12th. This manuscript was probably produced in a monastic house but for a lay reader. In style it is close to the *Ochsenhausen Psalter* (Paris, Bibliothèque Nationale). The two scenes shown are from the Life of Christ: at the top Mary leads Christ to school – an unusual subject – and below Christ is baptised by St John the Baptist.

Salome, about 1390

Spinello Aretino (1350/52-1410)

Italian (Arezzo and Florence)

Fresco, 39.5 x 31 cm

Formerly in the collection of William Roscoe

Presented by the Liverpool Royal Institution in 1948; inv. no. 2752

The fresco technique, in which paint is applied directly to wet plaster, was used for mural decorations throughout Italy from the 13th century onwards. This fragment comes from a destroyed chapel in the Florentine church of Santa Maria del Carmine, where it formed part of a scene showing the Feast of Herod in a cycle illustrating the life of St John the Baptist. The Gospel of St Matthew tells how Salome, the daughter of Herodias, danced seductively before the Jewish king Herod, who in return ordered the execution of the Baptist which Herodias demanded.

Mirror Case, about 1320

French

Ivory, diameter 13.3 cm

Presented by Joseph Mayer in 1867; inv. no. M8010

An elopement from a castle is shown in four scenes. The lady appears three times: being lifted down from the tower, being carried away on horseback, and (below) with her lover in a boat.

Christed Discovered in the Temple, 1342
Simone Martini (about 1284-1344)

Italian (Siena)

Tempera on panel, 49.6 x 35.1 cm

Formerly in the collection of William Roscoe

Presented by Liverpool Royal Institution in 1948; inv. no. 2787

When still a young child, Christ abandoned his parents during a visit to the Temple in Jerusalem and stayed behind to teach among the scholars there. His mother's words on finding him again are written in Latin on the book she holds: 'Son, why have you dealt with us like this?' The picture is signed and dated in Latin along the bottom edge of the frame: 'Simone of Siena painted me in the year of Our Lord 1342'. Simone was among the greatest artists of 14th-century Italy, but at this date he was working at Avignon in France, where the papal court was in exile from Rome. This sumptuous picture was presumably commissioned for private devotion by a high-ranking patron, possibly the pope himself. The jewel-like colours, the use of richly patterned gold, and the linear gracefulness of the figures are characteristic of the Gothic art of France as well as Italy. It is typical of Simone that these decorative qualities do not detract from the solemn emotional drama of the scene which is conveyed through gesture, pose and facial expression.

Pax, about 1450
Maso Finiguerra (1426-64)

Italian (Florence)

Silver niello, 5 x 8 cm

Presented by Joseph Mayer in 1867; inv. no. M61

Decorated with the Ascension of Christ. A pax was made for worshippers to kiss at Mass. It replaced the Kiss of Peace which they had given each other, but which was thought unseemly by about 1300. This pax is now set in a 19th-century silver frame.

The Virgin and Child with a Saint, about 1483-99

Bartolomeo Montagna (about 1450-1523)

Italian

Oil on panel, 37.8 x 36.5 cm

Purchased in 1978 with the help of the Art Fund; inv. no. 9375

Montagna was greatly influenced by Venetian artists such as Giovanni Bellini and did much of his work in Vicenza and Verona. The saint has been tentatively identified as St John the Baptist although it is unusual to depict an adult St John paying homage in this way to a Christ Child. In the past it has been suggested that the bearded figure was a portrait of Francesco II Gonzaga (1466-1519), ruler of Mantua, but the halo above the figure is original to the painting.

Three Studies for a Figure of St John the Baptist, between 1455 and 1499

Andrea Mantegna (1431-1506)

Italian

Brown ink on paper prepared with red chalk, 17.4 x 18.5 cm

Purchased from the Trustees of the Weld Heirlooms Settlement with the help of the Art Fund, the National Heritage Memorial Fund, Sir Denis Mahon and British Nuclear Fuels in 1995; inv. no. 1995.324

Mantegna, the leading artist in Italy at the time of his death, has quickly sketched out three different poses for a figure of St John the Baptist to whom a donor is appealing in prayer. The drawing was probably a study for an altarpiece and may have been linked to a painting commissioned in 1499 by Cardinal Georges d'Amboise, the archbishop of Rouen, who considered Mantegna the 'greatest painter in the world'. This sketch was one of the prize works in William Roscoe's large collection of drawings.

The Lamentation over the Dead Christ,
about 1486–87

Master of the Virgo inter Virgines (active about 1483–98)

Dutch (Delft)

Oil and tempera on panel, 55.2 x 56.3 cm

Formerly in the collection of William Roscoe

Presented by the Liverpool Royal Institution in 1948; inv. no. 1014

The anonymous Master of the Virgo inter Virgines was a leading artistic figure in the Northern Netherlands during the late 15th century. His name derives from one of his works which represents the Virgin and Child among four holy virgins (Rijksmuseum, Amsterdam). His works are distinguished by their austere colouring, emotional piety and ability to express overwhelming grief. The scene's poignant and horrific drama is emphasised by the desolate landscape and skull-like heads of the richly-dressed figures.

St Bernardino Preaching, about 1462–63
Studio of Lorenzo Vecchietta (1410–80)

Italian

Tempera on canvas transferred from wood, 30 x 76 cm

Formerly in the collection of William Roscoe

Presented by the Liverpool Royal Institution in 1948: inv. no. 2758

St Bernardino (1380–1444) was a Franciscan friar from Siena and the most important travelling preacher in early 15th-century Italy. He was canonised a saint in 1450. He is shown preaching from an outdoor pulpit on the façade of a church, which has been 'opened up' to reveal the interior. The artist's name is unknown. He was probably one of Vecchietta's talented associates working in Siena and may have been Francesco di Giorgio (1439–1501). He has used the new rules of perspective to focus attention on the crucifix at the centre of the composition. Following the custom of the time the women at the church service are divided from the men by a curtain.

Study of a Youth, about 1500
Luca Signorelli (about 1450–1523)

Italian

Black chalk with white gouache on paper, 41 x 21.5 cm

Presented by HM Government in 1981; inv. no. 9833

This magnificent study of a young apprentice is pricked along the figure edge and also 'squared up' to aid transfer up to a large scale. Drawings like this were kept on file in artists' studios and used as required to help compose both altarpieces and large wall frescoes.

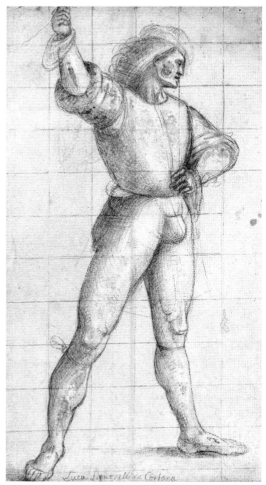

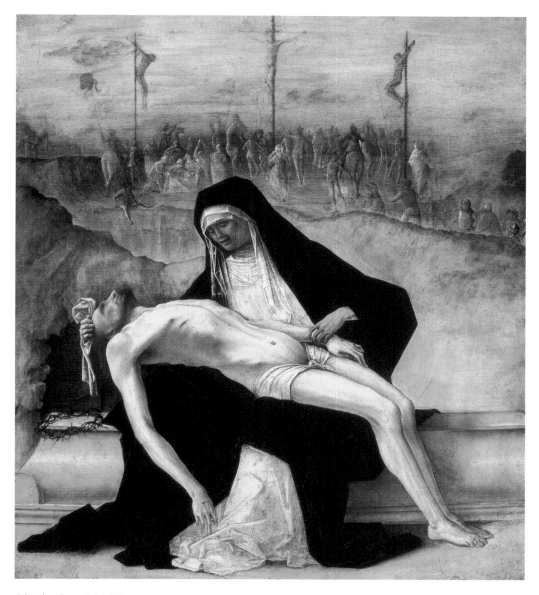

Pietà, about 1495

Ercole de' Roberti (about 1455/6-96)

Italian

Oil and tempera on panel, 34.4 x 31.3 cm

Formerly in the collection of William Roscoe

Presented by the Liverpool Royal Institution in 1948; inv. no. 2773

This centre predella panel is part of a large altarpiece that is still in the church of San Giovanni in Monte, Bologna. Originally the panel was positioned above the altar directly in front of the priest's face as he celebrated Mass. Pietà (Italian for 'piety') was a type of Northern European devotional subject that is without scriptural basis. Pietàs were imported into Italy from about 1450. Christ's unidealised blood-drained body, Mary's angular black cloak, her anguished face, and tender clasping of her dead son all combine to create an intense emotional effect. This is usually considered Ercole's masterpiece and is one of the finest of William Roscoe's pictures.

Altarpiece with Scenes from the Passion and Crucifixion, about 1496–1500

Master of the Aachen Altarpiece (active about 1485-1515)

German (Cologne)

Oil on panel, 109.1 x 54.2 cm, 106.8 x 54 cm (the two wings)

The wings were presented by the Liverpool Royal Institution in 1948; the central larger panel is on loan from the National Gallery, London (No 1049) The Crucifixion © The National Gallery, London. Presented by Edward Shipperdson, 1847); inv. nos. 1225, 1226

The left-hand panel showing Pilate washing his hands may include, in the man looking over Pilate's shoulder, a self-portrait of the artist, who is named after an altarpiece now in Aachen Cathedral. The backs of the wings show the Cologne mayor, Hermann Rinck, and his family at prayer in their private chapel. They are in front of a vision of Christ appearing at Mass and showing his wounds to the 6th-century saint, Pope Gregory the Great. The triptych was originally in the parish church of St Columba in Cologne.

1500–1700

The Walker's collection of 16th- and 17th-century Italian, Spanish and Netherlandish art is unusual among British public collections in its bias towards Mannerism. Like the medieval and early Renaissance holdings, the core of the collection of paintings and drawings of this period was formed by William Roscoe. The Walker owes to him the *Portrait of a Young Man* by Rosso Fiorentino and the drawing *Ulysses Shooting Through the Rings* by Rosso's Italian compatriot and rival at Fontainebleau Palace, Francesco Primaticcio. Roscoe's attraction to Mannerist art was probably related to his friendship with and support of the British-based Swiss artist Fuseli, whose anti-slavery sentiments he shared, and who greatly admired the work of Michelangelo and his Mannerist followers. At the beginning of the 19th century, when Roscoe was collecting, the Napoleonic Wars on the continent released on to the British market many works of art. *The Nymph of the Fountain* by Cranach, the most important German artist of the early 16th century, was in the hands of a Liverpool dealer by 1815, having 'been lately brought from the continent'.

Other additions to the Walker's drawings collection include Elisabetta Sirani's *Self-portrait* from the Weld-Blundell collection and a Guercino and a Ribera, both from the outstanding collection put together in the 18th century at Holkham Hall, Norfolk. Roscoe knew this well as he helped to catalogue its library for his friend, Thomas William Coke (1754–1842), later the Earl of Leicester. Examples of British Renaissance portraiture from the workshops of Holbein and Hilliard came from equally eminent collections. The *Portrait of Henry VIII* by Holbein's workshop had traditionally belonged to the family of Jane Seymour and was perhaps acquired by her brother Edward Seymour, 1st Duke of Somerset, leading courtier at the court of Henry VIII and Lord Protector of England during the early years of the reign of Edward VI.

The Walker's collection of 17th-century art is characteristic of the many British 18th- and 19th-century aristocratic collections from which the Gallery derives several of its more important paintings. This is especially so in its concentration of Dutch paintings, its focus on landscape art and its holdings of four prestigious Old Masters – paintings by Rembrandt, Rubens, Poussin and Murillo. All four of the Walker's paintings by these artists came from aristocratic collections as diverse as those of Charles I, the Duke of Devonshire, the Earl of Derby and Lord Overstone.

Landscape was one of the main genres of painting to develop in the 17th century. Poussin's *Landscape with the Gathering of the Ashes of Phocion* and the Dutch artist Ruysdael's *Landscape with a Ferry Boat* provide contrasting essays in landscape style – from Poussin's monumental austerity to Ruysdael's breezy naturalism. The lyrical landscape captured in the background of Elsheimer's *Apollo and Coronis* is enlivened with bright specks of paint suggesting beams of light skimming the tree tops and reflected in the pool.

Another 17th-century artist whose sentiment was particularly appreciated by British artists and collectors of later centuries was the Spanish painter Murillo. He was especially admired by artists such as Gainsborough for his mellow colouring, soft handling of paint and his charmingly tender representations of children, all of which chimed in well with the taste of the later 18th century and the first half of the 19th century.

*Scenes from the Life of
St John the Baptist,*
about 1505-10

**Circle of Francesco
Granacci (1469-1543)**

Italian (Florence)

Oil on panel, 77.4 x 228.6 cm

Bequeathed by PH Rathbone
in 1895; inv. no. 2783

Several incidents from the
saint's childhood are
combined in chronological
order from left to right. The
panel comes from a series
illustrating the life of the
Baptist - the patron saint of
Florence - which may have
decorated a private chapel in
the city. Other panels from
the same group are now in
the Metropolitan Museum of
Art in New York. The loggia
on the left is an elegant
example of Florence
Renaissance architecture,
and like the beautiful
landscape background it
gives the New Testament
figures a 16th-century Italian
setting.

Dish, 1500-20

Italian (Deruta)

Tin-glazed earthenware (maiolica), diameter 22.5 cm

Purchased with the help of the Friends of the National
Museums and Galleries on Merseyside in 1988;
inv. no. 1988.361

Renaissance designers were fascinated by the monsters of
Greek mythology and added their own improvements. It is often
uncertain, as with this piece, whether allegorical meaning was
intended.

Bearded Man in Armour, about
1515–20

**Master of Elsloo
(active 1500–about 1550)**

Dutch (Roermond)

Oak, height 165 cm

Purchased in 1963; inv. no. 6215

The sculptor is named after a major piece
of his in the Dutch town of Elsloo. The
figure wears a scallop shell breast-plate
and the Burgundian Order of the Golden
Fleece, and could represent a military
knight or ancestor figure. In the 19th
century the statue adorned the Great Hall
at Scarisbrick Hall, Lancashire.

St John the Baptist, about 1522–23

Antonio Correggio (probably 1489–1534)

Italian

Red chalk on pink prepared paper squared up in red chalk,
19 x 15.6 cm

Purchased from the Trustees of the Weld Heirlooms Settlement
with the help of the Art Fund, the National Heritage Memorial
Fund, Sir Denis Mahon and British Nuclear Fuels in 1995;
inv. no. WAG 1995.325

This drawing is Correggio's final study for the figure of St John
the Baptist in a fresco of the *Coronation of the Virgin* painted on
the apse ceiling of the Benedictine abbey of San Giovanni
Evangelista in Parma. It has been squared up to help the artist
paint it on a larger scale onto the half-domed apse. Correggio's
first inspiration as an artist came from Mantegna (see page 20).
The drawing was once owned by another artist, the American-
born Benjamin West, whose painting *The Death of Nelson* (see
page 69) is also in the Walker's collection.

Virgin and Child with Angels, about 1520–25

Joos van Cleve (about 1480s-1540/41)

Netherlandish (Antwerp)

Oil on panel, 85.5 x 65.5 cm

Purchased in 1981 with the help of the Art Fund and the National Heritage Memorial Fund; inv. no. 9864

Joos van der Beke (called Cleve after his native German region) can be documented as being in Antwerp from 1511. Joos and his workshop produced a large number of devotional panels depicting the Virgin and the Holy Family. He worked in a style typical of the Antwerp Mannerists using colourful and elaborate costumes, fluttering drapery and showy detail of plants, architecture and landscape. He was also one of the artists who introduced the Italianate style to the Netherlands. This painting reveals the influence of Leonardo, especially in the forms of the angels.

Triumph of Fortitude,
about 1525

Flemish (Brussels)

Wool and silk, 411 x 533 cm

Presented by Martins Bank Ltd in 1953; inv. no. 4115

The tapestry represents various male and female figures from mythology, classical and biblical history who showed fortitude. The design was one of a series of 'Triumphs' of the seven virtues. The tapestry may originally have been in a Spanish collection. Its Latin inscription in the upper border may be translated as: 'Virtue (enables) fearless hearts to oppose threatening dangers. In the same way salvation accepted from death pleases'.

Portrait of a Young Man, about 1530-40

Jan Mostaert (active 1475-1555/6)

Dutch

Oil on panel, 96.6 x 73.3 cm

Formerly owned by William Roscoe

Presented by the Liverpool Royal Institution in 1948; inv. no. 1018

In 1519 Mostaert was appointed court painter at Malines to Margaret of Austria, Governess of the Netherlands. He produced for her mainly portraits of the royal family, although most of his known pictures are of lesser members of the Dutch nobility, as probably is this portrait. He favoured a reserved dignified portrait style. He was also a good landscape painter, rendering his backgrounds in minute detail. In the background appears a conversion of St Hubert, who, while hunting on a holy day, saw a stag with a crucifix between its horns. The young man portrayed may have been called Hubert.

Portrait of a Young Man with Helmet,
about 1520–23

**Giovanni Battista di Jacopo, called Rosso Fiorentino
(1494-1540)**

Italian

Oil on panel, 88.6 x 67.3 cm

Formerly in the collection of William Roscoe

Presented by Liverpool Royal Institution in 1948; inv. no. 2804

Rosso Fiorentino was an expressive and eccentric exponent of
early Florentine Mannerism which was opposed to the balanced
compositions of the earlier Renaissance. The painting is signed
with the Latin form of Rosso's name - Rubeus - which probably
referred to the artist's red hair.

Portrait of Henry VIII, between 1537 and 1547

Workshop of Hans Holbein (1497/8-1543)

German

Oil on panel, 239 x 134.5 cm

Purchased in 1945; inv. no. 1350

Holbein, Henry VIII's court painter, created this archetypal image in 1537 for part of a wall-painting in Whitehall Palace (destroyed 1698), which showed the King with his parents and his third wife, Jane Seymour. This later copy was owned by the Seymour family. The innovative confrontational standing pose and the detailed observation of sumptuous costume and setting convey a powerful message of strength and majesty.

The Nymph of the Fountain, 1534

Lucas Cranach the Elder (1472-1553)

German

Oil on panel, 51.3 x 76.8 cm

Presented by the Liverpool Royal Institution in 1948; inv. no. 1223

The artist received his surname from his native city in Germany, where his father also worked as a painter. In 1505 Cranach moved to the court of the Elector Frederick the Wise in Saxony where he established a large workshop including his sons as assistants. The reclining female nude composition, based on an ancient text describing a fountain or spring guarded by a statue of a nymph, was repeated several times in Cranach's workshop. The Latin inscription on the fountain represents the lasciviously smiling nymph's words as she looks out at us through half-closed eyes: 'I, the nymph of the sacred fountain, am resting; do not disturb me'. This seductive nude characterises Cranach's mature style.

Ulysses Shooting Through the Rings, 1555–59

Francesco Primaticcio (1504–70)

Italian

Red chalk and white heightening on pink prepared paper,
24.3 x 32.4 cm

Formerly in the collection of William Roscoe

Purchased in 1991 with the aid of the Art Fund; inv. no. 10843

This finished drawing is a preparatory study for one of the 59
frescos relating the adventures of Ulysses which were painted
on the walls of the Ulysses Gallery at Fontainebleau Palace. The
drawing fulfilled both a practical function, providing
instructions to Primaticcio's assistants, and an aesthetic role as
an art object. Primaticcio's skill as a draughtsman and the
drawing's beauty attracted artists and connoisseurs. The
drawing was owned both by the painter, Joshua Reynolds, and
by the Liverpool collector, William Roscoe.

Queen Elizabeth I – 'The Pelican Portrait',
about 1574

Attributed to Nicholas Hilliard (1547-1619)

English

Oil on panel, 78.7 x 61 cm

Presented by E Peter Jones in 1945; inv. no. 2994

In this portrait of the Queen, aged about 41, she is treated
almost like a religious icon. Elaborate symbolism and rich detail
show off her status and queenly qualities, while her figure is
stylised and her face mask-like. The mother pelican on her
brooch is a traditional Christian symbol of Christ's sacrifice. It
was believed the pelican fed her young with her own blood –
here it refers to Elizabeth's role as mother of her people. Hilliard
was miniature painter to Elizabeth. This work relates closely to
his miniature portrait of 1572, but might be by a follower using
Hilliard's designs.

The Sacrifice of Noah, about 1576-77

Jacopo Bassano (about 1510-92)

Italian

Oil on canvas, 119.7 x 86.3 cm

Purchased with funds from the Wavertree Bequest in 1952; inv. no. 1219

This landscape is the right half of a larger painting from one of Jacopo Bassano's most popular series illustrating the biblical *Story of Noah* in four paintings. In the background Noah gives thanks to God for saving his family from the biblical flood. In the foreground his family build a house. Typical of Jacopo's paintings, the religious subject is surrounded by details of rural working life. Such naturalistic details appealed to art collectors in Venice and Jacopo's nearby native town of Bassano, after which he was named.

Apollo and Coronis, about 1606-1607

Adam Elsheimer (1578-1610)

German

Oil on copper, 17.9 x 23 cm

Presented by HM Government in 1982 from the estate of the 4th Baron Methuen; inv. no. 10329

Elsheimer was one of the most inventive artists on a small scale. His intricate compositions painted on copper inspired other artists, including Rembrandt and Rubens. This picture was reproduced in an engraving dedicated to Rubens, Elsheimer's friend. As was often the case with Elsheimer, his landscape mirrors and develops the subject's mood: the god Apollo picks medicinal herbs in a futile attempt to revive his unfaithful lover whom he had shot.

Table, about 1600

Italian (probably Rome)

Marble and *pietra dura* top, painted walnut and lime base, top 120.5 cm square

Purchased in 1991 with the help of the Art Fund; inv. no. 10839

Furniture inlaid with *pietra dura* (hardstone) was a perennial favourite with English visitors to Italy. This table was bought in the 19th century by Charles Winn or his son Rowland, first Lord St Oswald, for Nostell Priory, Yorkshire.

Plaque, 1600–25

Flemish

Silver-gilt, diameter 12 cm

Purchased in 1990; inv. no. 1991.22

The delicate chasing of the metal represents the *Adoration of the Magi*. The plaque was probably the centre of a larger piece of display plate such as a rosewater dish.

Self-portrait as a Young Man, about 1630

Rembrandt Harmensz. van Rijn (1606-69)

Dutch

Oil on panel, 69.7 x 57 cm

Presented by the Ocean Steam Ship Company acting as trustees of certain funds in 1953; inv. no. 1011

Rembrandt used his early self-portraits to explore the effects of light and to experiment with facial gesture. This self-portrait was the first painting by Rembrandt to enter a British collection. It was presented to King Charles I in the early 1630s by one of his courtiers, Sir Robert Kerr, Earl of Ancrum, who had acquired it after a diplomatic visit to The Hague in 1629. The painting remained in the Palace of Whitehall until the sale of the royal collection after the King's execution.

God the Father Supported by Angels, 1601–1606

Peter Paul Rubens (1577-1640)

Flemish

Red chalk and red ink with cream bodycolour on paper,
25.5 x 28.6 cm

Purchased from the Trustees of the Weld Heirlooms Settlement
in 1995 with the help of the National Heritage Memorial Fund,
the Art Fund, Sir Denis Mahon and British Nuclear Fuels;
inv. no. 1995.83

During Rubens' stay in Italy (1601–1608) he was greatly excited
by the work of Michelangelo amongst other Italian Renaissance
and classical artists. He returned to Antwerp with a mass of
copies including this drawing recording the figure of God from
Michelangelo's famous fresco of the *Creation of Adam,* painted
on the ceiling of the Sistine Chapel in Rome. Rubens later
touched up the figures to make them more muscular and
vigorous. He remained inspired by Michelangelo's art
throughout his career, keeping the copy drawings he had made
in his youth to stimulate his imagination. The drawing was later
owned by William Roscoe.

The Virgin and Child with St Elizabeth and the Child Baptist, 1630–35

Peter Paul Rubens (1577-1640)

Flemish

Oil on canvas, 180 x 139.5 cm

Purchased in 1960 with the help of the Art Fund; inv. no. 4097

Between 1600 and 1608 Rubens visited Italy and Spain. On his
return to Antwerp he was immediately recognised as the most
distinguished master in Flanders and was made court painter to
Archduke Albert, Regent of the Netherlands. He acted as
artistic and diplomatic ambassador to the Archduke, helping to
conduct peace talks between England and Spain. The two
children may have been modelled on his own sons by his second
wife, Helena Fourment, whom he married in 1630. Many copies
and variations, as well as engravings of this subject by Rubens,
attest to its enormous popularity.

Nude Holding a Curtain, about 1634

Giovanni Francesco Barbieri called Guercino (1591-1666)

Italian

Pen and ink, 20.3 x 24.3 cm

Purchased from Holkham Hall with the help of the Art Fund and the National Heritage Memorial Fund 1992; inv. no. 10849

The drawing was probably intended as a preparatory study for a painting, perhaps of Venus or another mythological lover. It may have been connected with the picture of Mars, Venus and Cupid of 1634 in the Galleria Estense at Modena. Guercino was one of the most accomplished draughtsmen of his time and was enthusiastically collected by connoisseurs throughout Europe.

The Magdalen, about 1630–39

Paulus Bor (about 1600-69)

Dutch (Amersfoort)

Oil on panel, 65.7 x 60.8 cm

Purchased in 1952; inv. no. 958

Although a contemporary of Rembrandt's, Bor favoured a different painting style that blended classical formalism with dramatic light effects, which he had learned from Caravaggio's work during his stay in Rome in the 1620s.

The Rape of Europa, about 1642

Bernardo Cavallino (1616-56)

Italian (Naples)

Oil on canvas, 101 x 133.7 cm

Presented by TA Hope in 1882; inv. no. 2771

The princess Europa is shown seated on a bull, the mythological god Jupiter in disguise, who is about to abduct her. Most of Cavallino's paintings of scriptural and literary subjects were probably intended for cultivated private patrons.

The Adoration of the Shepherds, about 1640–49

Jusepe de Ribera (1590–1652)

Spanish (Naples)

Black and red chalk with brown and black wash on paper, 16.5 x 19.5 cm

Purchased from Holkham Hall with the help of the Art Fund and Foundation for Sport and the Arts in 1992; inv. no. 10851

Ribera lived most of his artistic life in Naples where he prospered as painter to the region's Spanish viceroys and religious institutions. This fine drawing, which deftly combines coloured chalks with washes, is not related to a known painting, although the theme was a favoured one of Ribera's in the 1640s.

Landscape with the Gathering of the Ashes of Phocion, 1648

Nicolas Poussin (1593/4-1665)

French

Oil on canvas, 116.5 x 178.5 cm

Purchased with the help of the Art Fund and the National Heritage Memorial Fund in 1983; inv. no. 10350

Phocion was a great Athenian general and statesman of the 4th century BC. He was executed for treason on a false charge contrived by his political enemies and his body ordered out of Athens to Megara where it was burnt. In this painting a woman of Megara is carefully collecting the ashes and performing the appropriate ceremony over them. The grandeur of the subject is conveyed by the rigid structure, the geometrical organisation, the solidity and the perfect calm of the landscape and townscape. The fluctuations of fortune have led Phocion to an obscure burial in a foreign land but even there his austerity, rectitude and achievements are reflected in a classical, even heroic setting, dominated by the central temple and hill and by the dark massed trees on either side. Poussin turned to landscape in middle age, and this was one of the first of a group which virtually created a new tradition of classical landscape.

River Scene with a Ferry Boat, 1650

Salomon van Ruysdael (about 1600/3-70)

Dutch (Haarlem)

Oil on canvas, 106 x 152 cm

Bequeathed by EE Cook through the Art Fund in 1955; inv. no. 1022

Salomon van Ruysdael came from a family of artists, but little is known of his training. His paintings represent a calm, luminous world. Ruysdael was not concerned with producing a topographically exact view. Instead he brought together elements characteristic of the Dutch countryside to form an ideal yet naturalistic landscape.

Atalanta and Meleager, about 1658

Charles Le Brun (1619-90)

French

Oil on canvas, 212.5 x 280.5 cm

Presented by B Benjamin in 1852; inv. no. 2898

This is a cartoon (or preparatory painting) for one of a series of tapestries woven at the Gobelins factory, Paris illustrating the story of Meleager. Meleager killed the huge Calydonian boar which had been devastating his country, and here he presents its remains to Atalanta who had first wounded it.

The New Church at Delft with the Tomb of William the Silent, 1667

Hendrick Cornelisz. van Vliet (1611/12-75)

Dutch (Delft)

Oil on canvas, 127 x 85.5 cm

Purchased with the help of the Art Fund in 1994; inv. no. 1994.1

Van Vliet specialised in views of the interiors of Delft's two main churches, the Old and the New Church. The New Church housed the tomb of the assassinated Dutch hero, William I of Orange ('the Silent') (1533–84), who helped establish the independence of the Netherlands from Spanish rule.

Self-portrait, about 1664

Elisabetta Sirani (1638-65)

Italian

Red chalk on paper, 21.5 x 17.3 cm

Purchased from the Trustees of the Weld Heirlooms Settlement with the help of the Art Fund, the National Heritage Memorial Fund, Sir Denis Mahon and British Nuclear Fuels in 1995; inv. no. 1995.345

Sirani's artistic skill and beauty brought her European fame and female students. She fed the market for her celebrity with self-portraits such as this one, previously owned by the 18th-century curator of the Uffizi's self-portrait collection in Florence. His elaborately drawn frame surrounds the self-portrait. Sirani's early death, probably from stomach ulcers and overwork at the age of 27, increased her fame and aroused suspicions that she had been poisoned.

Virgin and Child in Glory, 1673

Bartolomé Esteban Murillo (1617-82)

Spanish (Seville)

Oil on canvas, 236 x 169 cm

Presented by the Art Fund in 1953; inv. no. 1351

This altarpiece was commissioned by Ambrosio Ignacio Spínola y Guzman, Archbishop of Seville (1670-84), along with a series of seven paintings of *The Life of St Ambrose* by Valdés Leal, for the archbishop's private chapel in his Seville palace. Spínola chose the most important religious artist in Spain to paint this grand but intimate image. During the Spanish Peninsular War (1808-14) the palace was the headquarters of the French marshal, Soult, who took the altarpiece with him as war booty to France without the central area of the canvas showing the appealing faces of the Virgin and Child. The two separated parts were not reunited until they were acquired by the British collector, Lord Overstone in 1862.

King Charles II, 1685

Godfrey Kneller (1646-1723)

German

Oil on canvas, 224.5 x 143 cm

Purchased in 1952; inv. no. 3023

Kneller came to England in 1676 and soon gained royal favour. Here the King's authority is subtly undermined: his face is stiff, his hand limp, and the crown and orb are hidden in shadow. Kneller presents an ageing and even lonely figure. This is the last of his portraits of Charles II, probably begun just before the King's death and finished afterwards.

Eighteenth-century art

Liverpool's growth from a minor estuary port to England's second city, which took place in the 18th and early 19th centuries, was matched by her development into one of the country's most significant provincial artistic centres. Outside the city, local landed patrons such as the Earls of Derby and Henry Blundell of Ince perpetuated an essentially aristocratic taste; but the access of mercantile wealth led to the emergence of both a new collector class and a local school of artists comparable to those which flourished in Norwich and Bristol. By the 1820s the Liverpool Academy, first mooted only a year after the foundation of the Royal Academy in London, was firmly established.

Wright of Derby's *Annual Girandola at the Castel Sant' Angelo,* presented in 1880, was almost the first significant 18th-century British painting to enter the Walker's collection. From then until the First World War, acquisitions in that sphere were dominated by the early Liverpool school and artists with strong local or north-western connections such as the Liverpool-born George Stubbs. The purchase of Stubbs' *Horse Frightened by a Lion* in 1910 was by far the Gallery's most outstanding achievement in the field of 18th-century British art for the best part of 60 years.

After the First World War early British art continued to be neglected until a watershed was reached in 1935. The purchase in that year of Richard Wilson's masterpiece *Snowdon from Llyn Nantlle* marked the Gallery's recognition that its holdings of 'classic' British art were inadequate, and the start of a policy of purchasing representative works by most of the leading 18th-century names. In the next 20 years, the Walker sought out first-rate examples of the conversation piece (by Devis, Zoffany and Gawen Hamilton); the society portrait (Ramsay, Romney, Cotes, Highmore); a classic horse-portrait by Stubbs (*Molly Longlegs*) and finally a magnificent example of that quintessentially British genre, the theatrical portrait, Hogarth's *David Garrick as Richard III.*

This 20-year period in mid-century provided an essential platform for the Gallery's most recent phase of collecting 18th-century art. Notable amongst the acquisitions are the great Gainsborough full-length of the first Countess of Sefton, portraits made in Liverpool by Wright of Derby and (remarkably) George Stubbs.

The Guitar Player, about 1700

Jacob van Schuppen (1670-1751)

French (Paris, Vienna)

Oil on canvas, 90.2 x 117.5 cm

Presented by the Liverpool Royal Institution in 1948; inv. no. 1195

Charmingly informal, this is probably a portrait of a courtier and his family painted before the artist left Paris in 1706-7. It may portray Sir William Waldegrave, a celebrated guitar player, who was doctor to the exiled British King James II in France. The guitar was popular at the French court in the early 18th century and was considered especially suitable for accompanying singing: the music book on the table appears to be open at a song. The prominence given to music-making is perhaps meant to suggest harmony within the family.

Amber Cabinet, about 1700

Polish (Gdansk)

Cabinet covered with pieces of amber and ivory, 45.7 x 35.7 x 25.1 cm

Purchased with the help of the Heritage Lottery Fund and the Art Fund with a contribution from the Wolfson Foundation in 2002; inv. no. 2002.12

Amber is fossilised tree resin, and Gdansk (formerly called Danzig) was the centre of the European amber trade at the start of the 18th century. The cabinet would have been owned by a very wealthy collector, who would have stored valuable treasurers inside it. Henry Blundell of Ince Blundell, north of Liverpool, acquired the cabinet shortly after 1800. It was repaired for him by the Liverpool sculptor and furniture-maker, George Bullock (see Candelabra, pages 70-71).

Ruins of Rome, about 1741

Giovanni Paolo Panini (1691-1765)

Italian

Oil on canvas, 173 x 221 cm

Presented by James Aikin in 1876; inv. no. 2794

Panini had a flourishing practice in Rome providing 18th-century Grand Tourists with souvenir composite views or *capricci*, like this of the most important ancient buildings in the city. Here are included Trajan's Column, the Pantheon and the Temple of Fortuna Virilis.

Mr and Mrs Atherton, about 1743

Arthur Devis (1711-87)

English

Oil on canvas, 92 x 127 cm

Purchased in 1940; inv. no. 1353

This portrait was once thought to have commemorated the couple's marriage in 1730, but is now believed to date from the following decade. William Atherton (died 1745) was sometime Alderman and Mayor of Preston, and a friend of the artist's father. Conversation pieces – family group portraits in an informal, domestic setting – were a distinctive feature of 18th-century British painting. The furniture shown in this work was almost certainly Atherton's own, but the rather palatial room and grand garden are probably inventions, designed to exaggerate their social standing.

Spring Clock, about 1720

Daniel Quare (1649-1724)

English

Ebony on oak case, gilded brass decoration, brass and steel movement, 33 x 22.5 x 14.5 cm

Purchased in 1968; inv. no. 1968.250

The striking movement has repeating work that will sound the time to the nearest quarter hour on two bells. Quare was one of the great clockmakers of his day; he invented repeating work for watches in about 1680.

David Garrick as Richard III, 1745
William Hogarth (1697-1764)

English

Oil on canvas, 190.5 x 250.8 cm

Purchased with the help of the Art Fund in 1956; inv. no. 634

David Garrick (1717-79) was the greatest British actor of the mid-18th century. He became famous from 1743 after his outstanding performance as Shakespeare's Richard III. He is shown here in the famous tent scene before the Battle of Bosworth, haunted by the ghosts of all those he had murdered. Garrick's body is contorted into a 'serpentine' line – a stretched 'S' shape that Hogarth considered distinctly beautiful and which he later made the basis of his theoretical treatise, *The Analysis of Beauty,* published in 1753. This first major Shakespearian picture is not just a portrait but also a grand history painting in which Hogarth emphasises England's importance. He believed that an incident from English history rather than ancient history could still be used to teach a moral lesson.

Two-handled Cup, 1744
Lewis Pantin

English

Silver-gilt, height 38 cm

Bequeathed by Lord Wavertree in 1933; inv. no. 3318

Made for display on a dining-room sideboard, this cup is fashioned in the swirling and asymmetrical rococo style.

Molly Longlegs, 1761–62

George Stubbs (1724–1806)

English

Oil on canvas, 101 x 126.8 cm

Presented by Lewis's Department Store, Liverpool in 1951; inv. no. 2389

Liverpool-born George Stubbs, the outstanding animal painter of the 18th century, gained an international reputation with the publication in 1766 of his *Anatomy of the Horse*. The picture, with its clear depiction of veins, bones and muscles, is among the best of his single horse portraits and indicates well how closely Stubbs' anatomical studies and portraiture interlinked. Molly Longlegs was a bay mare, who twice won 200 guinea prizes at Newmarket. She belonged to Lord Bolingbroke who probably commissioned the picture.

Snowdon from Lyn Nantlle, about 1765

Richard Wilson (1713-82)

Welsh

Oil on canvas, 101 x 127 cm

Purchased in 1935; inv. no. 2429

Wilson became a leading figure in British landscape painting as the first native artist who convincingly straddled the gap between the academic landscape and the topographical view. His models were the French 17th-century painters, notably Gaspard Dughet and Claude Lorrain, whose concern for the structure of a landscape, its sense of order, and feeling for light, are echoed in this masterpiece. Along with these guidelines Wilson has fused a marvellous sensitivity to location. His sense of design and tonal value gives the rugged grandeur of his native Welsh mountains a luminous and timeless repose.

Richard Gildart, 1768

Joseph Wright of Derby (1734-97)

English

Oil on canvas, 125 x 100 cm

Purchased in 1988; inv. no. 10637

Wright worked as a portraitist in Liverpool between 1768 and 1771. His presence had an enormous impact on the local art scene, and his works of this period reflected and helped to define taste in a burgeoning mercantile city. Gildart was one of Liverpool's most prominent citizens; a merchant in the sugar trade all his life, Mayor three times, Member of Parliament for nearly 20 years; and here 95 years old. Wright's formidable portrait is unflinching in its directness.

The Family of Sir William Young, about 1767-69

Johan Zoffany (1733-1810)

German

Oil on canvas, 114.5 x 167.5 cm

Purchased in 1937; inv. no. 2395

Previously dated to 1770 when Sir William Young (1725-88) obtained his baronetcy and was appointed Governor of Dominica, recent research has suggested a slightly earlier date for this painting. All the family wear theatrical Van Dyck costume, then very fashionable particularly in portraits. Musical instruments suggest the family enthusiasm for music. The presence of the black slave, John Brook, evokes their West Indian sugar plantations. Born and trained abroad, Zoffany arrived in London in 1760. In 1769 he was made a member of the Royal Academy by King George III.

Isabella, Viscountess Molyneux, 1769

Thomas Gainsborough (1727-88)

English

Oil on canvas, 236 x 155 cm

Presented by HM Government from the estate of the 7th Earl of Sefton in 1975; inv. no. 8780

Isabella Stanhope sat to Gainsborough at Bath early in 1769 shortly after her marriage to Viscount Molyneux. The artist had just been elected to the Royal Academy in London, and this work, sent soon afterwards to its first-ever exhibition, surely represents a deliberate effort to impress a London audience. The figure has a brilliant poise, and the play of light and shade on the satiny surface of her dress is a miracle of virtuoso painting. Shortly afterwards her husband was created the 1st Earl of Sefton, and the portrait hung at the Seftons' seat, Croxteth Hall near Liverpool, for two centuries until its acquisition by the Walker Art Gallery.

Horse Frightened by a Lion, 1770
George Stubbs (1724-1806)

English

Oil on canvas, 100.1 x 126 cm

Purchased in 1910; inv. no. 2387

Stubbs' principal reputation was as a horse portraitist. His aspirations to be considered a painter of loftier subjects led to the decision to paint his numerous *Lion and Horse* pictures. An antique Roman statue in the Palazzo dei Conservatori in Rome, showing a lion clawing at a horse's back, was seen by Stubbs when he visited the city in 1755 and almost certainly inspired the series. The horse, tense with fear, is depicted with magnificent anatomical precision. By contrast the lion, possibly painted from a skin, looks rather tame.

The Death of Cardinal Beaufort, 1772
John Henry Fuseli (1741-1825)

Swiss

Pen, ink, pencil and grey wash on paper, 65 x 81.9 cm

Presented by the Liverpool Royal Institution in 1948; inv. no. 1540

In Shakespeare's *Henry VI*, Cardinal Beaufort dies in black despair having been involved in the murder of Humphrey, the good Duke of Gloucester. Fuseli shows the young king, Henry VI, raising his arm and vainly demanding some sign of repentance from the Cardinal. The drawing was made in Rome and sent to England for exhibition. It combines Roman neoclassicism - the even lighting, flat composition and figures in rows - with the expressionist violence that was to characterise Fuseli's later more Romantic work.

Candelabra, about 1771

Matthew Boulton (manufacturer) (1728-1809)

English

Ormolu, height 46 cm

Purchased in 1980; inv. no. 1980.684

Probably one of each of the two pairs of 'lyon-faced' candlesticks bought at the Boulton sale at Christie's in 1772 by the Earl of Sefton. At his Soho factory in Birmingham Matthew Boulton pioneered the manufacture of high-quality gilt bronze, or ormolu, in England.

Commode, 1772

Giles Joubert (designer) (about 1689–1775)

French

Tulipwood and marquetry, 91 x 146 x 66 cm

Purchased in 1988; inv. no. 10774

One of a pair supplied by Joubert for the Salon de Compagnie of Mademoiselle du Barry (sister-in-law of Louis XV's mistress Madame du Barry) at Versailles. It is stamped RVLC for Roger Vandercruse Lacroix who manufactured it to Joubert's design.

Self-portrait, 1774

Anton Raphael Mengs (1728–79)

German

Oil on panel, 73.5 x 56.5 cm

Purchased in 1953; inv. no. 1227

In the best tradition of artists' self-portraits, this is a work of psychological insight. With the bohemian elegance there is also a sense of weariness – perhaps reflecting the huge demand throughout Europe for Mengs' religious and historical paintings. The artist points to a sketch for one of his last works, *Perseus and Andromeda*. It and this self-portrait were commissions from two of his many British admirers.

The Annual Girandola at the Castel Sant' Angelo, Rome, 1775–76

Joseph Wright of Derby (1734–97)

English

Oil on canvas, 138 x 173 cm

Presented by Robert Neilson in 1880; inv. no. 1428

Painted shortly after Wright returned from a trip to Italy, this was paired with the *Eruption of Vesuvius*: 'the one the greatest effect of Nature, the other of Art that I suppose it can be', he said. Wright was fascinated all his life with the powerful effects of light and made his name painting them. In his hands, the firework display held in Rome every Easter becomes an almost apocalyptic vision of the city.

Flock of Mountain Sheep with a Deciduous Tree,
1790s

Giovanni Domenico Tiepolo (1727-1804)

Italian

Grey ink and wash on paper, 23.5 x 18 cm

Bequeathed by George Palmer Holt, in 1990; inv. no. 1993.3

After the death of his artist father Giambattista Tiepolo in
1770, Domenico Tiepolo became Venice's leading painter until
his semi-retirement in 1785 to the family villa between Venice
and Padua. Thereafter he concentrated on drawing animals and
amusing caricatures of daily life. This drawing may be a study
for one of the series of frescoes of animals in landscape
settings which Domenico painted on the walls and over the
doors to decorate the villa. George Palmer Holt was the great
grandson of George Holt (1825-1896), who assembled the art
collection at Sudley House, another of the art galleries in the
care of National Museums Liverpool.

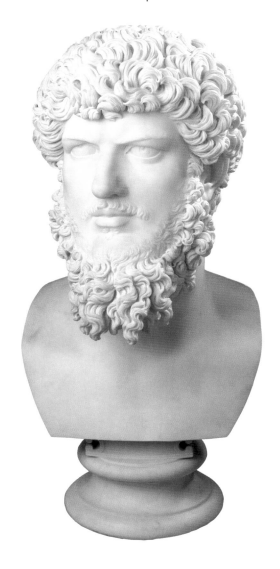

Bust of Lucius Verus, about 1777

Carlo Albacini (1739-1807)

Italian (Rome)

Marble, height 89 cm

Presented by Colonel Sir Joseph Weld in 1959; inv. no. 6538

Lucius Verus was a Roman Emperor of the second century
noted for his debauchery and profligacy. This is a copy of an
ancient bust now in the Louvre. It was bought from the artist by
Henry Blundell of Ince (near Liverpool) in 1777. Blundell formed
one of the largest collections of ancient sculpture ever
assembled in England, but he admired fine 18th-century copies
of classical works just as much as the originals. Much of
Blundell's antique sculpture is now in World Museum and his
17th- and 18th-century works are in the Walker.

Cup and Saucer, about 1775

Josiah Wedgwood (manufacturer) (1730-95)

English

Creamware, diameter 11.8 cm (saucer)

Presented by Joseph Mayer in 1867; inv. no. M276

Painted with views of Hawksmoor's mausoleum at Castle Howard (cup) and Stoke Gifford (saucer). In 1774 Wedgwood made a service painted with English views for Empress Catherine of Russia. These pieces are among the few other examples decorated in the same manner.

Interior of a Foundry, 1789

Léonard Defrance (1735-1805)

Belgian (Liège)

Oil on panel, 42 x 59.2 cm

Purchased with the help of the Art Fund, in 1990; inv. no. 10824

Defrance produced several paintings of foundries and forges in his native Liège, a town associated for centuries with metalworking and an important industrial centre by the late 18th century. This example is exceptional for the form of the artist's signature and the date, painted as if they are being cast in molten metal.

Nineteenth-century art

The Walker Art Gallery was founded in 1873 primarily to display and collect art of that period, and it is not therefore surprising that high and late Victorian art is represented there splendidly and comprehensively with a strong international flavour. Frederic Leighton's *Elijah in the Wilderness* could almost have been painted for a grand baroque 17th-century Roman church; Solomon J Solomon's *Samson* would surely have won a major prize at a 19th-century Paris Salon; and John Gibson's *Tinted Venus* can be compared with the work of many followers of Canova and Thorwaldsen.

Early Victorian art is less cosmopolitan but often more original. Millais' *Isabella,* with its intensity of symbolism and expressionism, is his first Pre-Raphaelite painting – the subject is doomed young love from Keats' poem of the same name and the composition is deliberately archaic. Ford Madox Brown's *Waiting* has a simple, modern, domestic subject, like so many early 19th-century British paintings, but treated with the religious fervour of early Flemish art. John Brett's *Stonebreaker* has a much less obvious symbolism but it is a supreme example in paint of Ruskin's belief in accurate rendering of every detail of the natural world.

The Liverpool contribution to early Pre-Raphaelitism is well represented by DA Williamson's intense and brilliant north Lancashire landscapes of the early 1860s. Later Pre-Raphaelitism was less sharply focused in technique and its emotional content was more sensual, more poetic, more dreamy – indeed there are clear links with the Aesthetic Movement. Burne-Jones' *Sponsa de Libano* depicts the passionate heroine of the Song of Solomon, while Albert Moore's later *A Summer Night* shows the artist moving away from pure form towards Pre-Raphaelite symbolism. The cult of Dante and of his love for Beatrice is well represented on a high poetic level by Rossetti's *Dante's Dream* and on a more prosaic and popular plane by Henry Holiday's *Dante and Beatrice*. Alone of the Pre-Raphaelites Holman Hunt remained faithful to early ideals and his *Triumph of the Innocents* – for all its supernatural imagery – still contains a realistically Palestinian peasant family on a journey with their ass.

Social realism was a very different movement but with its own ambiguity – Herkomer's *Eventide* is more than an indictment of Victorian workhouses and in Paris it was much admired by the Decadent critic JK Huysmans. Similarly, in sculpture Thornycroft's *The Mower* is both an ideal figure and the first life-size statue of an English farm labourer. Onslow Ford's *Peace* with its adolescent figure, naturalistic modelling and rich, detailed symbolic accessories is a more typical example of the 'New Sculpture'.

The Walker Art Gallery was fortunate in its leaders. Philip Rathbone, a younger son of one of Liverpool's leading merchant families, spent his early life in insurance but then became Chairman of the Gallery for most of its first 20 years. He combined a broad taste, embracing both Pre-Raphaelites and Naturalists, with a sharp eye for the young progressive artists of the Newlyn School and of the early years of the New English Art Club – although, always conscious of popular taste, he could also buy paintings like *And When Did You Last See Your Father?* by WF Yeames. A few avant-garde pictures also made their way into the collection. For example Segantini's *Punishment of Lust,* 1891, a Symbolist work, was bought in 1893 largely at the prompting of Rathbone, the then Chairman of the Walker Art Gallery Committee. The most important piece of Symbolist sculpture, *Mors Janua Vitae* by Gilbert, was a gift to the Gallery, as was Rodin's *Minerva*.

George Audley, who made his fortune from beer and whisky, was more active as a collector than as a member of the Walker Art Gallery's governing committee, and around the early 1920s bought for the Gallery late Victorian masterpieces at auction just when they were cheap and unfashionable. Liverpool is indebted to him for nearly all its paintings by George Clausen and for Stanhope Forbes's *By Order of the Court* as well as for about a further 50 notable mid- or late Victorian paintings. James Smith of Blundellsands (in north Liverpool), a wine merchant, was one of the most important patrons of GF Watts during the artist's later years. In 1877, the year that the Gallery opened, Andrew Kurtz, a local industrialist, commissioned for it Frederic Leighton's great *Elijah in the Wilderness* in order to establish proper standards for the future; in Victorian art at least he would not be disappointed.

Death of Virginia, about 1806-10
Giacomo de Maria (1762-1838)

Italian (Bologna)

Marble, height 214 cm

Purchased in 1968; inv. no. 6652

In Rome in the 5th century BC, one of the judges (*decemvirs*) conspired with a friend to kidnap and rape Virginia, the daughter of an army officer (or centurion). Her father found her eventually and stabbed her in order to preserve her chastity. Appalled by these events, the Roman people rebelled and abolished the arbitrary power of the *decemvirs*. The subject suited the revolutionary fervour of Napoleonic Italy and this group was carved largely for the instruction of the students at the Bologna Academy of Fine Art.

The Death of Nelson, 1806
Benjamin West (1738-1820)

American

Oil on canvas, 182.5 x 247.5 cm

Presented by Bristow H Hughes in 1866; inv. no. 3132

Crowds flocked when West exhibited this painting in his house a few months after the Battle of Trafalgar. Many of the portraits were said to be taken from life, but the event is presented in an idealistic and theatrical manner. The formula is similar to West's famous *Death of Wolfe,* which had revolutionised British history painting over 30 years earlier, but this work never enjoyed the same critical acclaim.

Linlithgow Palace, 1807
Joseph Mallord William Turner (1775-1851)

English

Oil on canvas, 91.4 x 122 cm

Presented from the FJ Nettlefold Collection in 1947;
inv. no. 2583

Linlithgow Palace to the west of Edinburgh, the birthplace of
Mary, Queen of Scots, was a romantic and picturesque ruin by
1807. Turner added naked nymphs and evenly balanced trees
that have the effect of elevating the picture above simple
antiquarian topography into something closer to a classical
history painting in the manner of Claude Lorrain. The thickly
impastoed sunlit clouds betray Turner's fundamental love of
depicting strong natural effects.

Pair of Candelabra (one of the pair shown), 1814-18
George Bullock (1782/3-1818)

English

Marquetry of rosewood and brass, with ebonised wood
mouldings and gilt metal mounts, height 198 cm

Purchased with the help of the Art Fund in 1989;
inv. no. 10781-2

Bullock was based in Liverpool between 1804 and 1814. These
candelabra were probably made after his move to London.
Following his sudden death they were purchased at the sale by
Sir William Gordon Cumming. They would have supported
candles or, more probably, oil lamps.

The Ruins of Holyrood Chapel, about 1824
Louis Jacques Mandé Daguerre (1787–1851)
French

Oil on canvas, 211 x 256.3 cm

Presented by Arnold Baruchson in 1864; inv. no. 3034

Daguerre specialised in painting dioramas. These were
realistically painted and illuminated giving a three-dimensional
effect and showing famous scenes or events. In this painting
we see a dramatic illusion of the chapel ruins by moonlight. The
picture has an almost cinematic impact, reflecting Daguerre's
dioramas. Later in life Daguerre experimented with
photography, and in 1839 he invented one of the first
photographic processes, the daguerreotype.

Venice, 1840

Joseph Mallord William Turner (1775–1851)

English

Watercolour on paper, 22.2 x 32.3 cm

Presented by RR Meade-King in 1934; inv. no. 999

One of a number of the limpid aquatic views of Venice from the so-called 1840 'Roll Sketchbook' that perfectly reveal Turner's commanding skill in old age as a water-colourist. Painted wet-on-wet, with subtractions of paint using sponge and scratching, the final surface notations are in rapidly applied red pen-strokes.

Napoleon Crossing the Alps, 1850

Paul Delaroche (1797–1856)

French

Oil on canvas 279.4 x 214.5 cm

Presented by Henry Yates Thompson in 1893; inv. no. 2990

In the summer of 1800 Napoleon, with a modest army, advanced into Italy and only about six weeks after leaving Paris totally defeated the Austrians at Marengo. Delaroche has selected from this great military campaign a very unremarkable incident – the Emperor crossing the Great Saint Bernard Pass on a mule borrowed from a local inhabitant and led by a Swiss peasant. In 1801 Jacques Louis David had painted a great flamboyant official portrait of Napoleon crossing the Alps on a rearing horse, pointing at the sky with his cloak swirling around in the wind. Delaroche's literal accuracy and careful detail – even in, for example, the mule's harness – show the gradual development of realism in the 19th century.

Faithful Unto Death, 1865
Edward Poynter (1836-1919)

British

Oil on canvas, 115 x 75.5 cm

Presented by Charles Langton in 1874; inv. no. 2118

This painting is a Victorian moral exemplar of absolute devotion to duty. The sentry stands at his post whilst Pompeii and its inhabitants are destroyed by the eruption of Vesuvius. Poynter's source was the excavation at Pompeii of the remains of a soldier in full armour, used as the basis for an imaginary incident in Bulwer-Lytton's popular historical novel *The Last Days of Pompeii* (1834).

The Tinted Venus, about 1851–56
John Gibson (1790-1866)

British

Tinted marble, height 175 cm

Purchased with the aid of V&A Purchase Grant Fund in 1971; inv. no. 7808

The Liverpool-trained Gibson was among the first neo-classical sculptors to paint his sculptures – it became generally known in the 19th century that this had been the practice in ancient Greece. His aim was not realism, as there is no attempt to simulate flesh colours, but his Venus was still denounced as 'a naked impudent English woman'. She carries the apple presented to her by Paris as the symbol of her beauty and power.

Elaine, 1870
Sophie Anderson (1823-1903)
British
Oil on canvas, 158.4 x 240.7 cm
Purchased in 1871; inv. no. 110

Elaine was the first work by a female artist to be bought for the future Walker Art Gallery's collection and was purchased before the Gallery was built. This remarkable acquisition indicates the forward-thinking attitude of PH Rathbone and the first purchasing committee. The painting depicts the fate of Lord Tennyson's heroine Elaine, an innocent country girl who falls in love with Sir Lancelot. He abandons her in favour of Queen Guinevere and she dies suffering from unrequited love. Anderson's picture depicts a servant rowing Elaine's body to King Arthur's palace at Camelot.

Speke Hall, No. 1, 1870
James McNeill Whistler (1834-1903)
American
Etching, drypoint, pen and pencil on paper, 22.4 x 14.9 cm
Purchased in 1975; inv. no. 9066

Between 1867 and 1877 Speke Hall, the Tudor mansion to the south of Liverpool, was the residence of the shipowner Frederick Leyland (1831-92). He was a patron of Whistler until they infamously fell out over the cost of Whistler's redecoration of Leyland's London house in 1876-77. Whistler stayed at Speke between 1869 and 1875, and produced a series of painted and etched portraits of Leyland, his mother, wife and daughters. This etching shows Leyland's increasingly estranged wife, Frances. The Walker owns several of the prints among its group of 34 Whistler etchings, a printmaking form of which he was a master.
(See page 10 for photograph of Whistler.)

Henry Wadsworth Longfellow, 1872

Edmonia Lewis (about 1844-1907)

American

Marble, height 68.5 cm

Accepted by HM Government in lieu of Inheritance Tax and allocated to National Museums Liverpool in 2003; inv. no. 2004.5

This bust portrays one of American's best-known cultural figures. Longfellow's poems, especially his *Song of Hiawatha* of 1855, shaped popular views of Native American culture. Edmonia Lewis was herself the daughter of a Native American (Chippewa) mother and an African American father. In Boston, where she started her sculpting career, she carved figures celebrating the American abolition of slavery. After moving to Rome, where she lived among a 'sisterhood' of female artists, she focused on Native American themes inspired by Longfellow's poems.

Flower Sellers of London, about 1875-76

Gustave Doré (1832-83)

French

Oil on canvas, 220.5 x 134.5 cm

Presented by Henry Thompson in 1880; inv. no. 2282

Doré first made his name in France in the 1850s and 60s as an illustrator of books and poems. His greatest achievement was the book *London: A Pilgrimage* (1872), illustrated with prints emphasising the gulf between high society and the grim life of the poor in the capital city. After his first visit to Britain in 1868 his paintings became particularly admired by the British. In 1873 Doré even accompanied the Prince of Wales on a fishing and painting holiday near Balmoral.

Elijah in the Wilderness, 1877-78

Frederic Leighton (1830-96)

British

Oil on canvas,
234.3 x 210.4 cm

Presented by AG Kurtz in 1879: inv. no. 147

The prophet Elijah is fleeing from Jezebel who is scheming to kill him. In this painting he is asleep in the wilderness and an angel from God is bringing him bread and water. The angel seems to have just landed, his splendid wings still extended, but the prophet, his magnificently muscled nude body contrasting with the fluttering draperies of the angel, still lies asleep, as the angel looks tenderly down on him. This is one of the greatest academic paintings of the Victorian era.

Athlete struggling with a Python, first cast 1877; this cast 1910

Frederic Leighton (1830-96)

British

Bronze, height 98.5 cm

Purchased in 1910; inv. no. 4155

Leighton frequently made small sculptures as models for his paintings but this was his first large independent bronze group. Its vigorous modelling, varied surfaces and very naturalistic pose marked a decisive break with the neo-classicist style still prevalent in late Victorian sculpture. This figure was much admired by certain young sculptors, such as Edward Onslow Ford, whose work became known as the 'New Sculpture'.

Eventide: a Scene in the Westminster Union, 1878

Hubert von Herkomer (1849-1914)

British

Oil on canvas, 110.5 x 198.7 cm

Purchased in 1878; inv. no. 751

Originally drawn by Herkomer as a magazine illustration, the subject is the bleak interior of the St James Workhouse, Westminster, an institution for female paupers. Paintings drawing attention to social problems such as poverty, homelessness and unemployment were unusual in Victorian art, but a number of social realist pictures were exhibited amidst some controversy in the 1870s.

Cabinet, about 1878

James Lamb (1817-1902)

British

Ebony veneered, inlaid with silver, 150 x 230 x 50 cm

Purchased in 1992; inv. no. 1992.61

This is probably the cabinet exhibited by the Manchester firm at the Paris International Exhibition of 1878, where they won a gold medal.

And When Did You Last See Your Father? 1878

William Frederick Yeames (1835-1918)

British

Oil on canvas, 131 x 251.5 cm

Purchased in 1878;
inv. no. 2679

This is an imaginary scene set during the English Civil Wars in a Royalist house occupied by the Parliamentarians. The artist was inspired to paint it by the innocent and candid character of a young nephew who lived with him. The suspense of the subject and the simplicity of the composition made it very popular, particularly in waxworks and in history textbooks of the mid-20th century. It has become the archetypal Victorian narrative painting and its title is often used to caption newspaper cartoons.

Peacock (about 1873 to 1880)

Made by Minton, Stoke-on Trent

Majolica earthenware, height 154 cm

Originally in Liverpool Town Hall, acquired by the Walker Art Gallery in 1891;
inv. no. 3985

Majolica was inspired by Italian Renaissance ceramics of the 15th century and was developed by Leon Arnoux (1816–1902), Minton's art director. The bright colours, which could be produced in Majolica ceramics, were very popular in the 19th century. This peacock was modelled by Paul Comolera (1818–97). Only 12 peacocks were ever made by Minton.

Hope, about 1879

George Frederic Watts (1817-1904)

British

Oil on canvas, 66 x 53.3 cm

Bequeathed by James Smith in 1923; inv. no. 2105

Hope sits on a globe representing the world. She strains to hear the music of the one string left in her lyre. This is a sketch for a larger painting at Tate Britain. Watts thought highly of the Walker's earlier version, and gave it to his friend Frederic Leighton whose art is well represented in the Gallery's collection (see page 76). US President Barack Obama used a sermon titled 'The Audacity of Hope' to inspire his election campaign. The sermon explained how Watt's figure of Hope can inspire people today.

Tomb Effigy of the Duchess of Nemours, 1881–83

Henri Michel Antoine Chapu (1833-91)

French

Marble, 53.5 x 229 x 91.5 cm

Purchased in 1994 with the aid of the Art Fund; inv. no. 1994.129

The Duchess of Nemours (1822–57) was a close friend and cousin of Queen Victoria and Prince Albert. She died in exile with other members of the French royal family at Claremont, near Weybridge, Surrey, where she was buried in a specially built chapel attached to the Roman Catholic church of St Charles Borromeo. Her husband commissioned her tomb from Chapu, one of the main French academic sculptors of the second half of the 19th century. Chapu's naturalistic work influenced several British sculptors of the period.

Off to the Fishing Grounds, 1886

Stanhope Alexander Forbes (1857-1947)

British

Oil on canvas, 119.5 x 156 cm

Purchased in 1886; inv. no. 2914

Forbes led a generation of British artists who painted outdoors. In 1884 he moved to the village of Newlyn in Cornwall to take advantage of the wonderful light and the chance to live among the subjects of his paintings. Several artists had already settled there but Forbes became their leader. Their work focused on the life of the small fishing community. This painting shows the men of Newlyn at work on board a Cornish lugger, a traditional fishing boat.

The Mower, about 1882–94

**William Hamo Thornycroft
(1850–1925)**

British

Bronze, height 190.5 cm

Purchased in 1894; inv. no. 4136

This is probably the first important life-size statue of a manual labourer in Britain. It reflects the desire of the artists of the 'New Sculpture' to widen their repertory in the direction of naturalism and of everyday life. Indeed, the sculptor was inspired by seeing a mower at work on the river banks during a Thames boating trip. All the same, the figure is also a carefully arranged image of thought and reflection plainly inspired by Donatello and associated by the sculptor with a quotation from Matthew Arnold's poem *Thyrsis*.

The Shepherdess, 1885

George Clausen (1852–1944)

British

Oil on canvas, 64.7 x 46 cm

Presented by George Audley in 1932; inv. no. 434

Clausen's early paintings follow closely the principles of the French artist Jules Bastien-Lepage, whose work was much admired in the early years of the New English Art Club. The girl's rather awkward pose – and her colossal boots – suggest an authentic peasant atmosphere. This is enhanced by the way the landscape rises up sharply behind her, seeming to enclose her within it. The grey light and carefully varied focus and brush strokes are further elements of this style. The painting was first owned by John Maddocks of Bradford, the most important patron of Clausen and of other progressive artists of the 1880s.

Samson, about 1886–87

Solomon Joseph Solomon (1860–1927)

British

Oil on canvas, 244 x 366 cm

Presented by James Harrison in 1887; inv. no. 3131

Samson, having lost his strength when Delilah cut off his hair, is being bound by the Philistines. Delilah, on the right, mocks him. Here is a young British artist trained in Paris and anxious to demonstrate his command of those academic skills highly valued there – anatomy above all, but also expression, grouping and pose.

A Summer Night, about 1885-90

Albert Moore (1841-93)

British

Oil on canvas, 132 x 228.5 cm

Purchased in 1890; inv. no. 2125

Moore's paintings were informed by the study of Greek sculpture and Japanese art, and by the idea of 'art for art's sake'. His rhythmically posed female figures, combined with decorative accessories, were vehicles for the exploration of an abstract language of form, colour, line and pattern. A *Summer Night* shows four women preparing for sleep on a luxurious balcony overlooking a moonlit lagoon. Despite the deliberate lack of story or allegorical meaning, a note of eroticism, common in the artist's late work, is evident.

Peace, 1887-89

Edward Onslow Ford (1852-1901)

British

Bronze, height 183 cm

Purchased in 1891; inv. no. 4213

Peace is represented by a young girl with a dove and the palm branch of victory, standing on the armour of war. All the symbols are individually conventional enough. However, giving them to a very naturalistically modelled nude young girl in an unusual and vivacious pose is an example of the new approach to allegory for which the 'New Sculpture' was famous.

My Thoughts Are My Children, 1894
George Frampton (1860-1928)

British

Bronze, framed in wood, overall size 333 x 116 cm

Presented by Meredith Frampton in 1984; inv. no. 10461

George Frampton was an exponent of the 'New Sculpture', a movement in late 19th-century British sculpture whose followers favoured naturalistic modelling but often chose symbolic or mysterious subject matter. In this work a mother and her children are shown among swirling clouds or draperies above the hovering figure of a young woman. The meaning is unclear, and the whole composition has the look of a dream or apparition. Frampton derived his technique of modelling in low relief from Italian Renaissance sculptors such as Donatello, whose work he greatly admired.

Minerva, 1905–1907
Auguste Rodin (1840-1917)

French

Marble and bronze, height 48 cm

Bequeathed by James Smith in 1923; inv. no. 4181

A whole series of busts of Minerva designed in 1896 were inspired by Rodin's friendship with Mrs Mariana Russell, wife of the Australian painter, John P Russell. The use of different materials within the same sculpture to achieve textural variety became very popular in the late 19th century.

The Punishment of Lust, 1891

Giovanni Segantini (1858-99)

Italian

Oil on canvas, 99 x 172.8 cm

Purchased in 1893; inv. no. 2127

As Segantini moved towards Symbolism around the end of his life, he became attracted by a Buddhist poem, *Nirvana*, written by Luigi Illica. The poem describes the gradual redemption of mothers guilty of abortion or child neglect, achieved by their painful passage through a dismal icy valley. Nirvana (or final expiation) is presumably represented by the distant splendid mountain range painted from the Swiss Alps near St Moritz. The artist was protesting at the emancipation of women from their traditional role as mothers.

Mors Janua Vitae, about 1905–1907

Alfred Gilbert (1854-1934)

British

Painted plaster and wood, height 170.2 cm

Presented by E Percy Macloghlin in 1909; inv. no. 4230

The title means: 'Death, the door to life'. This is a model for a tomb commissioned by Eliza Macloghlin for her husband Percy, a provincial doctor, and for herself; their ashes were to be placed in the casket clasped by husband and wife. They were both atheists and so the symbolism is pagan not Christian, with Anteros (selfless love) on the left lower panel and Eros (sexual love) on the right – this must refer to their mutual love. The monument itself (in bronze) is in the Royal College of Surgeons in London but it was on this model that the sculptor himself worked with its brilliant, ghostly colour and its rich, fantastic detail.

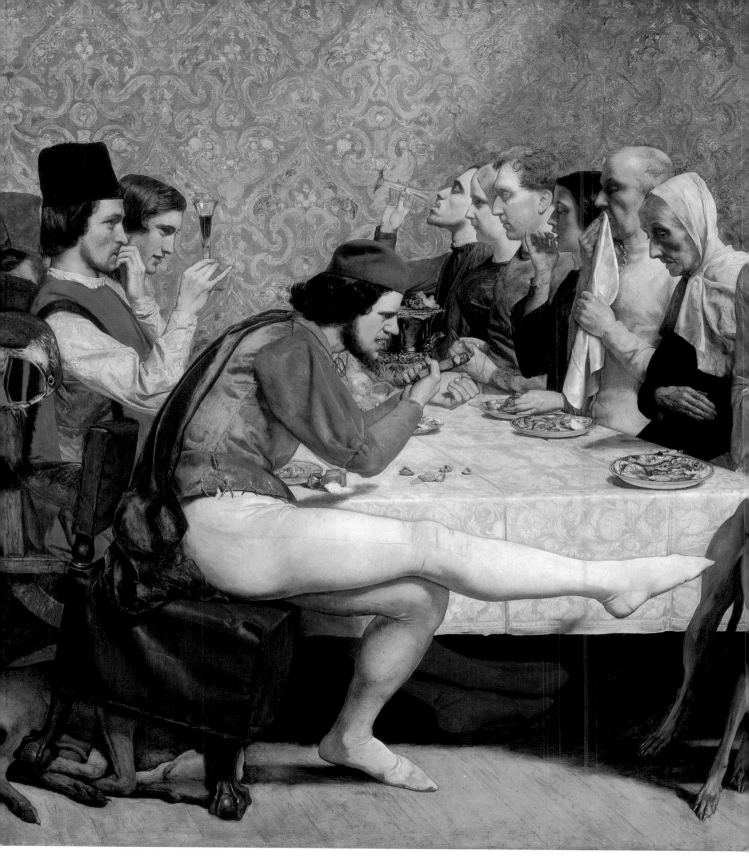

The Pre-Raphaelites

Isabella, 1848–49

John Everett Millais (1829–96)

British

Oil on canvas, 103 x 142.8 cm

Purchased in 1884; inv. no. 1637

One of the very first paintings in the new Pre-Raphaelite style, *Isabella* was begun shortly after the foundation of the Pre-Raphaelite Brotherhood in 1848, when Millais was only 19. The harshly brilliant colour combined with sharp detail, the deliberately unbalanced composition and the self-conscious angularity and flatness were all controversial features of Pre-Raphaelitism, loosely inspired by early Italian painting. The subject was taken from a poem by John Keats, itself derived from a story by the 14th-century Italian writer, Boccaccio, about the love between Isabella, the sister of wealthy Florentine merchants, and their poor, low-born apprentice Lorenzo. The jealous brother (on the left) later murdered Lorenzo, but Isabella found his body, cut off the head and buried it in a pot of basil which she watered with her tears; the ending is foreshadowed by the pot of herbs in the background. The highly individualised faces include a portrait of Millais' friend and fellow Pre-Raphaelite Brother, Rossetti (rear centre), drinking from a wineglass.

Self-portrait, 1850
**Ford Madox Brown
(1821–93)**

British

Black chalk on paper,
25 x 23 cm

Purchased in 1984;
inv. no. 10505

Brown drew this self-assured portrait of himself whilst completing his enormous painting *Chaucer and the Court of Edward III* (Art Gallery of New South Wales, Sydney) for exhibition at the 1851 Royal Academy. He was 29 years old, and by this time, although not an official member of the Pre-Raphaelite Brotherhood, he had made lasting friendships with its leaders Rossetti, Holman Hunt and Millais.

Waiting: an English Fireside of 1854–55, 1851–55
Ford Madox Brown (1821–93)

British

Oil on panel, 30.5 x 20 cm

Purchased in 1985 with the aid of the National Heritage Memorial Fund, the Pilgrim Trust and the Friends of National Museums and Galleries on Merseyside; inv. no. 10533

The woman is waiting for her soldier husband to return from the Crimea: his portrait miniature is on the table. The artist's wife and daughter posed for the picture. This everyday scene in an ordinary middle-class room lit by limelight and firelight has been painted with a quiet intensity, suggesting a Madonna and child in modern dress.

The Stonebreaker,
1857–58

John Brett (1831–1902)

British

Oil on canvas, 51.5 x 68.5 cm

Bequeathed by Mrs Sarah Barrow in 1918; inv. no. 1632

This painting is a tour-de-force of Pre-Raphaelite truth to nature. The boy is knapping flints for road-making, a task often given to paupers. His figure and clothing, the plants, the rocks, the sky, the shadows and every detail of the distant Surrey landscape are transcribed with scientific accuracy, reflecting Brett's interest in the writings of John Ruskin.

Spring, Arnside Knot and Coniston Range of Hills from Warton Crag, 1863

Daniel Alexander Williamson (1823–1903)

British

Oil on canvas, 27 x 40.6 cm

Bequeathed by James Smith in 1923; inv. no. 784

The early work of this Liverpool-born painter showed little awareness of Pre-Raphaelitism. In 1861 he moved to Warton-in-Carnforth in North Lancashire, where he painted a series of small, vibrant Pre-Raphaelite-influenced landscapes, remarkable for their luminous colour.

Sweethearts and Wives, 1860

**John J Lee
(active 1859-67)**

British

Oil on canvas, 84.5 x 71.3 cm

Purchased with the aid of the
V&A Purchase Grant Fund,
the Art Fund, the Friends of
the National Museums and
Galleries on Merseyside and
private donations in 1980;
inv. no. 9753

Scenes showing soldiers or
sailors parting from their
families were common in the
Victorian period. These
sailors are departing to take
up duties on HMS *Majestic,* an
obsolete 80-gun, ex-Crimea
wooden warship, anchored in
the Mersey as part of the
port defences. In 1863, she is
recorded as having
prevented two American
Confederate battleships
from leaving Laird's shipyard
in Birkenhead. John Lee, like
Windus, Davis and other
Merseyside painters, came
under the influence of the
London Pre-Raphaelites.
Very little is known about his
life. Only four of his paintings
can be identified with
certainty and three of these
are in the Walker Art Gallery.

Dante's Dream, 1870–71 & 1879

Dante Gabriel Rossetti (1828-82)

British

Oil on canvas, 216 x 312.4 cm

Purchased in 1881; inv. no. 3091

Rossetti had a life-long interest in the Italian poet, Dante. This painting represents an episode from the *Vita Nuova* in which Dante dreams that he is led by Love to the deathbed of Beatrice Portinari – the object of his unrequited passion. In this, his largest ever painting, Rossetti creates a visionary world using soft rich colours and complex symbols: the attendants wear green for hope, the spring blossoms signify purity, the red doves the presence of love, the poppies the sleep of dreams and death. The model for Beatrice was Jane Morris, with whom Rossetti had a long-term affair.

The Triumph of the Innocents, 1876–87

William Holman Hunt (1827–1910)

British

Oil on canvas, 157.5 x 247.7 cm

Purchased in 1891; inv. no. 2115

Joseph is shown leading Mary and the infant Christ on their nocturnal flight into Egypt. They are accompanied by the souls of the innocent children massacred by Herod. Garlanded in flowers, the children are borne along on a visionary stream of bubbles, symbolic of the promise of the millennium following the coming of the Messiah. Hunt gives a typically unorthodox interpretation to a traditional story from the Bible. He uses complex symbolism and authentic settings and costume, based on what he had seen on his several visits to the Holy Land. *The Triumph of the Innocents* was Hunt's last major Biblical subject.

Madonna Pietra degli Scrovigni, 1884

Maria Spartali Stillman (1843-1927)

British

Watercolour and bodycolour on paper, 77.1 x 58.1 cm

Presented on behalf of subscribers by Harold Rathbone in 1884; inv. no. 923

The subject of this watercolour is a poem by Dante, which was translated by the Pre-Raphaelite artist, Dante Gabriel Rossetti. It describes the poet's love for a beautiful but aloof lady, dressed in green. Stillman was a pupil of the Pre-Raphaelite artist, Ford Madox Brown. She also sat as a model for other members of the Pre-Raphaelite circle including the painters Edward Burne-Jones, Dante Gabriel Rossetti and the successful female photographer, Julia Margaret Cameron.

Dante and Beatrice, 1882–84

Henry Holiday (1839-1927)

British

Oil on canvas, 142.2 x 203.2 cm

Purchased in 1884; inv. no. 3125

At his death Holiday was described as 'the last Pre-Raphaelite', and this picture was probably in part inspired by Rossetti's several Dante subjects. Dante is shown being ignored by Beatrice (but not by her companions) as they pass him near Santa Trinita Bridge in Florence.

Sponsa de Libano, 1891

Edward Burne-Jones (1833-98)

British

Gouache and tempera on paper,
325.7 x 158 cm

Purchased in 1896; inv. no. 113

Based on the biblical *Song of Solomon,* this shows
the North and South winds blowing, as requested
by King Solomon, upon his bride of Lebanon.
Despite this being a rather voluptuous Biblical
episode, Burne-Jones emphasises the languorous
dream-like and chaste nature of the bride,
surrounded by lilies, which are symbolic of virginity.
Burne-Jones' figure-style is inspired by Botticelli
and the flat and decorative linear treatment is like
stained glass or tapestry. An earlier tapestry design
was the basis for this picture.

Echo and Narcissus, 1903

John William Waterhouse (1849-1917)

British

Oil on canvas, 109.2 x 189.2 cm

Purchased in 1903; inv. no. 2967

The unhappy nymph Echo was condemned to repeat the last words spoken to her. She fell in love with the beautiful youth Narcissus, but he rejected her and was punished by falling in love with his own reflection. Waterhouse was of a younger generation than Rossetti and Burne-Jones, and his subjects of doomed and unhappy love were prettier, less disturbing and more widely popular than theirs.

ELEANOR.F.BRICKDALE

The Little Foot Page,
1905

**Eleanor Fortescue-
Brickdale (1872-1945)**

British

Oil on canvas, 90.8 x 57 cm

Presented by an anonymous
donor in 1909; inv. no. 1723

Fortescue-Brickdale was an
admirer of the Pre-
Raphaelites and adhered to
their early style despite
beginning her career in the
late 1890s. The foliage in this
painting shows her
unwavering dedication to
their principle of 'Truth to
Nature', in which everything,
including each blade of grass,
was painted in minute detail.
In a letter to the Gallery the
artist admitted that 'there is
no particular story to tell in
[this picture] ... but that a girl
dresses up as a page boy in
order to follow her lover on
his adventures'.

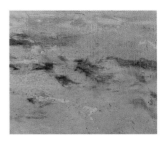

Impressionists and Post-Impressionists

Conservative taste by Liverpool Council's arts committee and a lack of money prevented the acquisition of Impressionist and Post-Impressionist pictures by the Walker until about 1935, other than a Le Sidaner in 1911. The appointment of Frank Lambert to the directorship of the Gallery in 1931 and the £20,000 given in the Wavertree bequest marked the beginning of a less timid purchasing policy. Lambert admired the paintings of Sickert and British Post-Impressionist artists, particularly Gilman, Gore, Bevan and the 'Camden Town' painters, who specialised in depictions of everyday intimate interiors and metropolitan street views. Lambert bought Gilman's *Mrs Mounter* – usually considered his masterpiece – and acquired by purchase and gift four outstanding Sickerts.

Lambert's successor, Hugh Scrutton, concentrated on buying representative late 19th-century French paintings: between 1959 and 1968 pictures by Monet, Cézanne, Vuillard, Seurat, Sargent, Courbet and Degas were purchased – usually with the help of substantial grant-in-aid from various government agencies and from local benefactors. Fortunately, Impressionist pictures were not then being sold for the high prices they now obtain.

The purchase of Tissot's *Portrait of Mrs Catherine Smith Gill and Two of Her Children* in 1981 brought back to Liverpool the only picture by one of the French Impressionist circle to have been painted in the city. Tissot was a political refugee in England for some years and in 1877 visited Liverpool to paint Mrs Gill at her home in Woolton – in the same year that the Walker Art Gallery opened.

Low Tide at Trouville, 1865

Gustave Courbet (1819-77)

French

Oil on canvas, 59.5 x 72.5 cm

Purchased in 1961 with the help of the Art Fund; inv. no. 6111

The great French realist painter was profoundly moved by the sea and returned to it as a subject at regular intervals. He concentrated on immense expanses of sea and sky, reducing incident to a minimum and creating an essay in subtle tonal modulation. With this and similar paintings, Courbet and his friends, Boudin and Whistler, brought the seascape into the modern era, and provided a distant but direct antecedent for colour-field abstract painting in the 20th century.

The Murder, about 1867-70

Paul Cézanne (1839-1906)

French

Oil on canvas, 65.4 x 81.2 cm

Purchased in 1963 with the help of the Art Fund; inv. no. 6242

Early in his career Cézanne painted a group of works depicting violent themes. This image may have been derived from a popular broadsheet. The dark tone and vigorous handling of the paint, along with the contorted bodies and faces of the figures, reinforce the desperate and menacing nature of the subject.

Portrait of Mrs Catherine Smith Gill and Two of Her Children, 1877

James Jacques Joseph Tissot (1836-1902)

French

Oil on canvas, 152.5 x 101.5 cm

Purchased in 1979 with the help of the Art Fund; inv. no. 9523

Catherine Smith Gill, wife of a Liverpool cotton-broker, is portrayed with two of her children, Robert and Helen. The setting is Lower Lee in Woolton, a Liverpool suburb. Tissot exhibited with the Impressionists, settled in England after 1870, and was a friend of the Gill family.

Woman Ironing, about 1890

Edgar Degas (1834-1917)

French

Oil on canvas, 80 x 63.5 cm

Purchased in 1968 with the help of the Art Fund; inv. no. 6645

Degas' laundress pictures paralleled his more famous ballet dancer series, and for both he studied the precise movements of women at work. The art of Degas was that of a 'Naturalist', depicting what was considered vulgar - laundresses were commonly perceived as borderline prostitutes - in a way that was almost scientific. A double viewpoint is used - looking straight at the woman's face, and down at her board. Her outlined and cropped figure also indicate Degas' debts to both Japanese art and snapshot photography.

Ville d'Avray, White Houses, 1882

Georges Pierre Seurat (1859-91)

French

Oil on canvas, 33 x 46 cm

Purchased in 1961 with the help of the Art Fund; inv. no. 6112

This oil sketch, depicting the countryside outside Paris, dates from Seurat's early career. It shows the artist's growing interest in scientific colour theory and the Divisionist technique with which he painted scenes in small patches and dots of pure colour.

Break-up of the Ice on the Seine near Bennecourt,
about 1892–93

Claude Monet (1840–1926)

French

Oil on canvas 65 x 100 cm

Purchased in 1962; inv. no. 6133

A wintry early morning view towards two of the narrow islands
of trees at Bennecourt near Giverny on the River Seine. By 1890
Monet complemented his on-the-spot Impressionist practice
with extensive studio re-working. This resulted in many
pictures with close-toned atmospheric harmonies, most
famously in his Rouen Cathedral and haystack series, but
nonetheless still evident in this painting.

The Viaduct at Arcueil, between 1898 and 1900

Henri Matisse (1869-1954)

French

Oil on canvas, 35.5 x 28 cm

Purchased in 1964 with the help of the V&A Purchase Grant Fund;
inv. no. 6216. © Succession H. Matisse/DACS 2018

Arcueil was an outer suburb of Paris where Matisse regularly painted street
scenes, such as this view of its railway viaduct, between 1898 and 1900. In
1899, during his honeymoon in London, Matisse was inspired by the
experimental use of colour in Turner's art. On his return to Paris he began to
explore colour more fully, applying high-keyed anti-naturalistic colours with
freer brushstrokes. By 1905 he had further developed this Post-Impressionist
style, which was nicknamed Fauvist (like a wild beast). Matisse, along with his
rival Picasso, came to dominate modern art in the 20th century.

Madame Hessel on the Sofa, 1900–1905

Edouard Vuillard (1868-1940)

French

Oil on board, 54.6 x 54.6 cm

Purchased in 1964; inv. no. 6217

Lucie Hessel and her picture-dealing husband were close friends of Vuillard. Madame Hessel is shown relaxing in her rue de Rivoli apartment, surrounded by pictures that are by Cézanne, Renoir, Lautrec and Vuillard himself. Vuillard used a distinctive dry brushstroke, and the cardboard itself under the paint contributes to line, modelling and shadow.

St Paul's from the River. Morning Sun in Winter, 1906–1907

Henri Le Sidaner (1862-1939)

French

Oil on canvas, 90 x 116 cm

Purchased from the Liverpool Autumn Exhibition in 1911; inv. no. 2373

Le Sidaner's paintings, like those of his friend the Impressionist Monet, capture the fleeting effects of light on water and buildings. This painting shows his fascination with the view of St Paul's dome, seemingly floating above the city of London. Unlike the Impressionists Le Sidaner did not paint outdoors, instead working from memory and small sketches, and enlarging them onto canvas in the studio. Like some Post-Impressionist artists he believed that art should do more than copy nature; it should also express moods and emotions.

Bathers, Dieppe, 1902

**Walter Richard Sickert
(1860-1942)**

British

Oil on canvas,
131.4 x 104.5 cm

Purchased in 1935;
inv. no. 2262

Sickert's viewpoint, without a horizon and with the daring off-centre positioning of figures, is intended as an immediate, almost snapshot, capture of a glimpse of reality. Strongly influenced by his friend Degas, Sickert was the most powerful of British artists working in the Post-Impressionist idiom. This and several other pictures were made as interior decor for a Dieppe café, but the patron disliked them and sold them off.

Vespers, 1909
**John Singer Sargent
(1856-1925)**

American

Oil on canvas, 71 x 91.5 cm

Presented by George Audley in 1928; inv. no. 2634

Rapid, dazzling brushwork made Sargent the outstanding portrait painter of his day. His virtuoso technique is here applied to a landscape, painted during a visit to Corfu in 1909. The painting is akin to the work of the French Impressionists in its spontaneity and rendering of sunlight.

Under the Hammer, about 1914
**Robert Bevan
(1865-1925)**

British

Oil on canvas 63.7 x 91.7 cm

Purchased in 1933; inv. no. 112

Bevan loved horses and they were the subject of most of his paintings. This picture of a horse fair includes Bevan and his daughter Edith, in the centre, and his wife Stanislawa, on the left. He admired the work of Paul Gauguin and other Post-Impressionist painters. Like them he used flat blocks of solid colour and strong outlines in his paintings.

Mrs Mounter, 1916/17

**Harold Gilman
(1876-1919)**

British

Oil on canvas 91.8 x 61.5 cm

Purchased in 1943;
inv. no. 3135

Mrs Mounter, the artist's fellow tenant and cleaning lady at 147 Maple Street, London, was the subject of several of Gilman's drawings and paintings. This sympathetic portrait brightens the colours of a rather ordinary interior, creating a striking, patterned effect. Mrs Mounter's face becomes a patchwork of colours which reflect surrounding surfaces. Gilman was a close friend of Sickert and was strongly influenced by Post-Impressionist painters, particularly the works of Van Gogh and Gauguin.

Twentieth-century and contemporary art

Gallery director, Frank Lambert, staged a large exhibition of modern prints and drawings at the Walker in March 1938, which included works by Picasso, Matisse, Dalí and Klee. He also added a major Surrealist display within the 1938 Liverpool Autumn Exhibition, but it was not until well after the Second World War that the Gallery gave any serious attention to the purchase of more modern continental pictures. Its only Picasso, a drawing, was presented as late as 2000. Virtually all purchases were of British art. Even moderately 'modern' British works caused difficulties and in 1938 the Arts and Libraries Committee voted against the purchase of a Paul Nash painting. Nash's work was not to join the collection until 1947 when his important painting *Landscape of the Moon's Last Phase* was presented by the Contemporary Art Society.

The Walker Art Gallery served as the local food office between 1939 and 1950 – although even in those dark days it bought Lowry's *The Fever Van* in 1943 – and it reopened to the public with no regular exhibition of national contemporary art. In 1957, however, thanks to the enlightened sponsorship of Sir John Moores, the first John Moores Liverpool Exhibition was held, aiming 'to give Merseyside the chance to see an exhibition of painting and sculpture embracing the best and most vital work being done today throughout the country' and 'to encourage contemporary artists, particularly the young and progressive'.

Sir John Moores was himself an amateur artist and he was particularly keen on this second aim; in the 1950s neither the London dealers nor the Royal Academy gave a warm welcome to progressive art and the John Moores Exhibitions rapidly attained pre-eminence among advanced artists and art critics. The jury was changed each exhibition and included such distinguished figures in the early years as Sir John Rothenstein (1957), Sir Alan Bowness (1959), André Chastel (1959), Sir William Coldstream (1963) and Clement Greenberg (1965). More recent jurors have included Tracey Emin, Jake and Dinos Chapman and Sir Peter Blake, the latter announced in 2011 as the exhibition's first Patron. Stylistic uniformity in the exhibitions was thus avoided and each exhibition has presented a new challenge to artists, to critics and to the public.

Prizes were awarded and some of these were purchase prizes, enabling the Walker Art Gallery to build up its collection of contemporary art with an assurance and an authority which had not been possible since the early years of the Autumn Exhibitions. Jack Smith's *Creation and Crucifixion* won the major purchase prize at the first exhibition in 1957; Hockney's *Peter Getting Out of Nick's Pool* received the first purchase prize in

1967; Peter Doig's *Blotter* came from the 1993 exhibition and the tradition still carries on today, with the exhibition renamed as the John Moores Painting Prize. Like the exhibitions the acquisitions have covered a wide stylistic range, reflecting the taste of very different juries. Peter McDonald's *Fontana*, the winner in 2008, and Keith Coventry's *Spectrum Jesus,* the winner in 2010, are the most recent works to join the collection through the John Moores.

The Walker has not confined its purchases of contemporary art to this route. Over the past decade in particular the Gallery has sought actively to broaden the representation of different media within the collection, beyond painting, to better represent the diversity of contemporary artistic practice. The acquisition in 2004 of Bill Viola's video installation *Observance* signalled a commitment to add major examples of 'new media' work to the collection. The purchase of Helen Chadwick's major suite of photographs, *Viral Landscapes*, in 2006 and Louise Bourgeois' *Ears*, a drypoint print with embroidery on cloth, purchased in 2005, are also emblematic of the pursuit to develop the collections beyond more traditional media. The Chadwick and Bourgeois also reflect the Gallery's aim to strengthen its holdings of work by women artists, and, in the Viola and Bourgeois, to bring a more international perspective to the contemporary holdings.

Bust of Alfred Wolmark, 1913
Henri Gaudier-Brzeska (1891-1915)
French
Bronze, height 67.3 cm
Purchased in 1954; inv. no. 4113

This bust of the painter Alfred Wolmark was made at the time that Gaudier was connected with Wyndham Lewis' 'Vorticist' movement. The sculpture, with its exaggerated facets of face and hair, is redolent of machinery surfaces and cog-wheels.

Portrait of Pau Cucurny with a Dog, 1903
Pablo Picasso (1881-1973)
Spanish
Brown ink and blue watercolour on paper, 21.5 x 12.8 cm
Given by an anonymous donor in 2000; inv. no. 2000.34
© Succession Picasso/DACS, London 2018

Paul Cucurny (known as Pau in Catalan) was a middle-class art enthusiast, who probably first met Picasso in the Barcelona bar-restaurant *Els Quatre Gats* (The Four Cats). This quickly sketched portrait may well have been drawn in the bar, as the dog looks like one owned by the bar owners. The bar closed in June 1903 and Cucurny died shortly afterwards. In 1903 Picasso was very poor, but he was also painting what are now considered masterpieces of his Blue Period (1901-1904). He used mainly sombre blue pigments, often to depict destitute people.

1932 (prince & princess)

Ben Nicholson (1894–1982)

British

Oil on board, 29.5 x 46.7 cm

Purchased in 1993 with the help of the Art Fund and of the Friends of the National Museums and Galleries on Merseyside; inv. no. 1993.78

Inspired by the table-top still lifes of the Cubists, this picture has an autobiographical significance: the profiles on the playing cards are those of the artist and the sculptor Barbara Hepworth, with whom he was sharing a studio at this date. The emphasis on surface texture, the playful use of line and the flattening of realistic space show the artist moving from representation towards the lyrical semi-abstract compositions for which he is best known.

The Fever Van, 1935

Lawrence Stephen Lowry (1887-1976)

British

Oil on canvas, 43.1 x 53.5 cm

Purchased in 1943; inv. no. 363

© The Estate of LS Lowry. All rights reserved, DACS 2018

An ambulance in a narrow street collects a diphtheria or scarlet fever sufferer. Lowry's views of working-class Salford where he collected rents have become nostalgic icons of a now defunct northern industrial city life.

Two Jamaican Girls, 1937

Augustus John (1878-1961)

British

Oil on canvas, 76.2 x 63.8 cm

Purchased in 1938; inv no. 3140

© The Estate of Augustus John/Bridgeman Images

Augustus John taught drawing in the School of Architecture and Applied Art at Liverpool University from 1901 to 1902. His flamboyant character caused a stir in the city, and is reflected in the vivid, unconventional works with which he later made his name as a portrait painter. In this portrait, painted in Jamaica, the rapid brush work of the dresses and the bright vibrant colours contrast with the girls' slightly sombre expressions. John's attention is concentrated on the sitters' heads and their subtly distinct characters.

Mirrored Glass Panel, 1939

Made at The London Sand Blast Decorative Glass Works

Peach-tinted mirrored glass panel, cut, acid-etched and sandblasted, 76 x 76 cm

Purchased in 1987; inv. no. 1987.139

The design of this panel represents Neptune. It is one of 15 panels, which originally formed the face of a wall-mounted clock in the first-class dining room of the second *Mauretania*. Only 13 panels still exist and nine of these are on display in the Walker's Craft and Design Gallery. The central panel represents the sun and contained the clock face. The surrounding glass panels represent planets of the solar system.

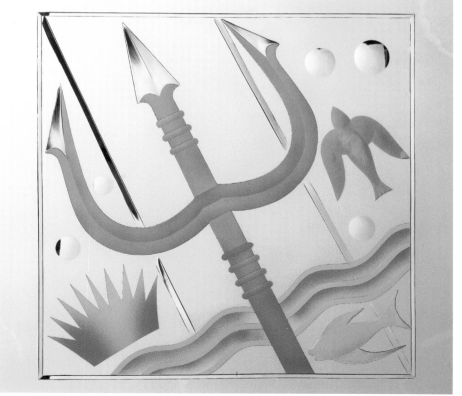

Landscape of the Moon's Last Phase, 1944

Paul Nash (1889-1946)

British

Oil on canvas, 63.5 x 75.8 cm

Presented by the Contemporary Art Society in 1947;
inv. no. 3143

This view of Wittenham Clumps, Berkshire, features regularly in Nash's late mystical landscapes which follow in the English Romantic tradition of Samuel Palmer and William Blake. The sun, the moon and the changing seasons became personal symbols of life and death, while the place itself, the site of an ancient earthwork, evokes man's primitive past.

Interior at Paddington, 1951

Lucian Freud (1922-2011)

British

Oil on canvas, 152.4 x 114.3 cm

Presented by the Arts Council in 1951; inv. no. 3134

© The Lucian Freud Archive/Bridgeman Images

The model, Harry Diamond, was a friend of the artist. He spent six months posing for the picture. Freud creates a mood of depression and neglect, while his unrelenting scrutiny of every detail and the figure loitering outside add to the sense of unease. Freud said 'the task of the artist is to make the human being uncomfortable'.

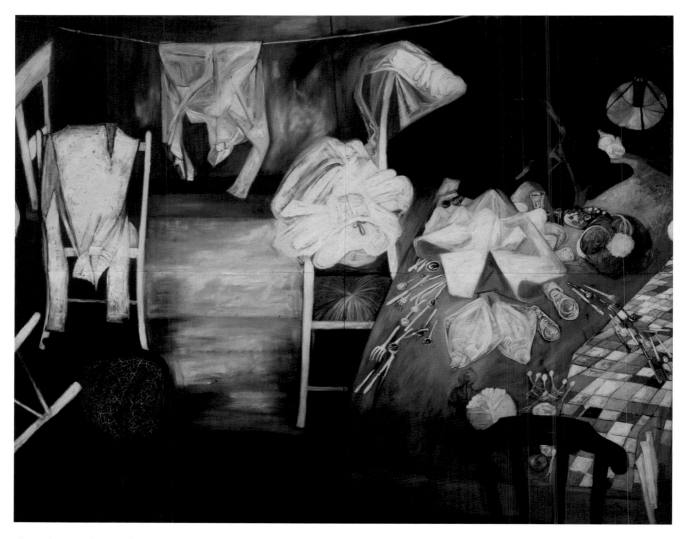

Creation and Crucifixion, 1955–56

Jack Smith (1928-2011)

British

Oil on hardboard, 243.8 x 304.3 cm

Presented by Sir John Moores in 1957; inv. no. 1236.
Copyright Estate of Jack Smith, Courtesy of Flowers Gallery

The deliberately mundane interior suggests a link to 'kitchen-sink' realism. This was denied by the artist, who wrote: 'my concern at that time was to make the ordinary seem miraculous'. The painting won first prize at the first of the biennial series of John Moores Liverpool exhibitions held in 1957.

Falling Warrior,
1956–57

Henry Moore (1898-1986)

British

Bronze, 63.5 x 147.5 x 78.5 cm

Purchased in 1961;
inv. no. 5598

Reproduced by permission of
The Henry Moore Foundation

Moore wrote: 'I wanted a figure that was still alive... a figure in the act of falling and the shield became a support... emphasising the dramatic moment that precedes death'. His figure, one of eleven cast, fuses landscape rock and natural forms with naked body.

Hermaphrodite, 1963

Allen Jones (born 1937)

British

Oil on canvas, 213.5 x 122 cm

Purchased in 1963; inv. no. 6190

© Allen Jones

Several of Allen Jones' prints, sculptures and paintings explore the tension between male and female. These two fused figures express the Jungian notion that truly creative art requires both feminine and masculine characteristics. It is thus a metaphorical self-portrait of Jones' own artistic quest. The overtly erotic female imagery is characteristic of much of Jones' subsequent art.

Peter Getting Out of Nick's Pool, 1966

David Hockney (born 1937)

British

Acrylic on canvas, 213.4 x 213.4 cm

Presented by Sir John Moores in 1968; inv. no. 6605

In 1966 Hockney travelled to Los Angeles for the second time. Attracted by the sunny climate and the relaxed atmosphere of West Coast America, he began to record characteristics of the lifestyle there in a series of paintings based on the theme of the swimming pool. Here, Hockney's friend Peter Schlesinger is depicted climbing out of the pool of Nick Wilder, a Los Angeles gallery owner. The painting is a composite view. Schlesinger did not actually model in the water; the pose derives from a snapshot of him leaning against an MG sports car. The white border and square format of the work are reminiscent of the Polaroid prints Hockney used as studies for the composition.

Still life: Autumn Fashion, 1978

Patrick Caulfield (1936-2005)

British

Acrylic on canvas, 61 x 76.2 cm

Purchased in 1979; inv. no. 9590

Caulfield's eclectic pictorial vocabulary borrows from Cubism, comic book outlines and highly detailed magazine photography. Although he often parodied kitsch or clichéd images, his pictures are usually the result of highly schematic and almost traditional composition. Caulfield did not consider himself to be a 'Pop' artist, although he is often categorised as such.

Broken Bride 13.6.82, 1982

John Hoyland (1934-2011)

British

Acrylic on cotton duck, 254 x 228 cm

Presented by Sir John Moores in 1982; inv. no. 10365

Hoyland's principle in this work, which won the John Moores first prize in 1982, was to build up the structure through formal contrast. Individual colours, shapes and textures achieve force and luminosity when seen against adjoining areas. The painting is both cerebral and sensual, underpinned by an instinctive search for radiance and harmony.

Viral Landscapes, No. 2, 1988-89

Helen Chadwick (1953-96)

British

C-Print photographs, powder coated steel, aluminium, plywood and Perspex, 120 x 300 cm

Purchased from the Helen Chadwick Estate with the help of the Art Fund in 2006; inv. no. 2006.1

© The Estate of Helen Chadwick and David Notarius

Chadwick was a pioneer of feminist art and one of the most influential British female artists of the 20th century. This is one of a series of five photographic montages entitled *Viral Landscapes*. They were made in the late 1980s when AIDS was provoking artists to explore the nature of viruses. Chadwick expressed her ideas using her own body, digitally placing images of some of her cells, including cells from her cervix and kidneys, onto photographs of ancient rugged coastlines. She highlights both a virus's capability to colonise the body and our colonisation of the natural world.

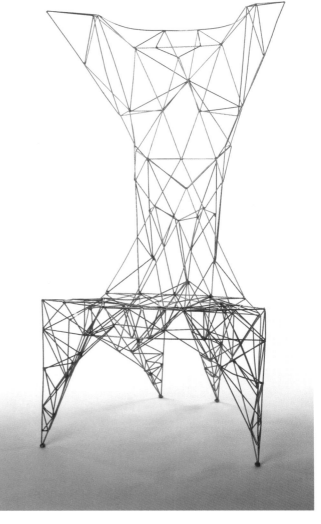

Pylon chair, 1991-93

Designed and made by Tom Dixon (born 1959)

British

Steel wire, 132 x 66 x 56 cm

Purchased in 1995; inv. no. 1995.27

Courtesy of www.tomdixon.net

Tom Dixon welded together steel wire to create a light, but also a very stable and strong, chair. He was inspired by the intricate frame drawings seen in computer-aided architectural designs. Initially made in his workshop, the Pylon chair design was later manufactured by the Italian company, Cappellini.

Blotter, 1993

Peter Doig (born 1959)

British

Oil on canvas, 249 x 199 cm

Presented by the John Moores Family Trust in 1993;
inv. no. 1993.81

Blotter won the 1993 John Moores exhibition, and Doig went on to be nominated for the Turner Prize in 1994. He based this painting on a photograph of his brother standing on a frozen pond, taken in Canada where they were brought up. Although it appears a simple outdoor scene, like much of his work it is also mysterious. The water pumped over the ice enhances the reflections, adding to the painting's surreal atmosphere. The ambiguous title portrays the figure's absorption in the landscape, the paint soaking into the canvas, and possibly hints at drug-related slang.

In the Comfort of the Bonnet, 2001–2002

Paula Rego (born 1935)

British

Coloured lithograph on paper, 98.5 x 73 cm

Purchased in 2004; inv. no. 2005.12

Paula Rego is one of Britain's foremost living artists. She is a staunch feminist and her art is directed towards the injustices suffered by women, including in her native Portugal. This print is a portrait of Jane Eyre from a series of 25 loosely based on Charlotte Brontë's 1847 novel. Jane's aged face, her slumped posture and use of her bonnet to cradle her head make her appear depressed. It possibly represents her dejection towards the end of the novel as she discovers she cannot marry her beloved Mr Rochester.

Observance, 2002

Bill Viola (born 1951)

American

Still from colour high-definition video on plasma display mounted on wall, 120.7 x 72.4 x 10.2 cm

Purchased with the help of the Art Fund in 2004; inv. no. 2004.24

Observance is one of Viola's most poignant works and is based on Dürer's altar wings *Four Apostles* (1526) in Munich. Viola creates a modern interpretation of a spiritual evocation of shared grief. Viola asked his cast to line up and in turn face the camera, confronting an imagined situation they would 'rather not see'. Their personal reactions create a composition of great depth and intensity.

Performers: Alan Abelew, Sheryl Arenson, Frank Bruynbroek, Carol Cetrone, Cathy Chang, Ernie Charles, Alan Clark, JD Cullum, Michael Irby, Tanya Little, Susan Matus, Kate Noonan, Paul O'Connor, Valerie Spencer, Louis Stark, Richard Stobie, Michael Eric Strickland, Ellis Williams
Photo: Kira Perov

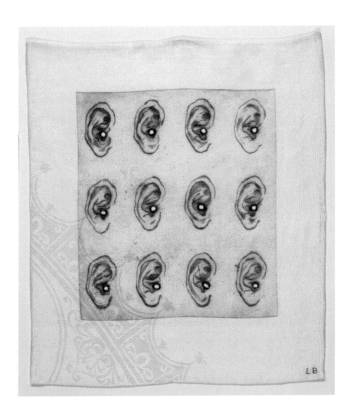

Ears, 2004
Louise Bourgeois (1911-2010)
American

Drypoint printed onto cloth and embroidery, 45.3 x 37.5 cm

Purchased from Marlborough Graphics with the help of the Art Fund in 2005; inv. no. 2006.2

© The Easton Foundation/DACS, London/VAGA, NY 2018

Paris-born Bourgeois was one of the most innovative American artists of the 20th century, working as a painter, sculptor and printmaker. Her work became known in Britain after her giant sculpture of a spider was shown at Tate Modern in 2000. *Ears* shows 12 subtly different images of her own ear printed and embroidered onto a napkin taken from her wedding trousseau. They symbolise Bourgeois' desire to understand others and reveal her need to avoid isolation.

Fontana, 2006
Peter McDonald (born 1973)
British

Acrylic gouache paint on canvas, 81 x 114.2 cm

Purchased with funds from the Friends of National Museums Liverpool and the Frederick W Mayor Bequest in 2009; inv. no. 2009.2

© Peter McDonald

Peter McDonald was born in Tokyo but studied in London. Of his work he says: 'My paintings depict a colourful world... They have a cartoon-like simplicity and waver at the point where figuration might tip at any moment into abstraction.' In his opinion he is representing a utopia, a vision of a simplified world. This painting won the John Moores Painting Prize in 2008. The title and the image of this work are a reference to the painter Lucio Fontana, who was renowned for slashing his canvases with a knife.

Index of artists